St. George's Cooks

St. George's Cooks

A Collection of Recipes from
The Nevil Memorial Church of
St. George
and
The Children's Ark

The Nevil Memorial Church of St George
Ardmore, PA

Published By
The Nevil Memorial Church of St George
Box C, 1 West Ardmore Avenue
Ardmore, PA 19003

In association with
CASEMATE
2114 Darby Road
Havertown, PA 19083

ISBN 1-932033-29-7

Cataloging-in-publication data is available from the Library of Congress

Typeset and Design by Casemate

First Edition, First Printing

PRINTED AND BOUND IN THE UNITED STATES OF AMERICA

CONTENTS

This cook book is dedicated to the memory of Chris Smythe.
A good Christian, a valued member of St. Geroge's Congregation,
and an excellent cook.

Acknowledgements

This cook book was prepared by a committee of members of the congregation of St. George's chaired by Karen Schloesser. Members include: Donna DiPaulo, Claire & Richard Coyle, Kate Gibbons, Eileen Kammerer, David Farnsworth, Liz Havens, Franciso & Jennifer Robelo and Bryn Thompson.

Chapter Artwork by Wendy Havens-Fasbinder

Cover Photographs by Bob Hamilton

Recipes were provided by current and former members of St. George's Church and by families of children attending The Children's Ark at St. Georges.

Cover Design by Mousemat Design, Orpington, Kent, UK

Printing by McNaughton & Gunn, Saline, MI

<u>All proceeds from the sale of St. George's Cooks will go to St Georges Church</u>

St. George's Cooks

*St. George's Episcopal Church is a stately stone structure located at
1 West Ardmore Avenue in Ardmore, Pennsylvania, just outside of Philadelphia
in an area referred to as the Main Line.*

In preparation for our 75th Anniversary in 2007, St. George's congregation began reflecting on its traditions, values and history. One tradition quickly popped to the forefront. Eating!

At St. George's we love to eat. And we love to prepare all our celebrations ourselves. For our Easter Vigil, we serve roast lamb and all the trimmings for more than 150 guests. At our annual Holiday Festival there's a reception featuring wines and heavy hors d'oeuvres, plus breakfast, lunch, tea and a bake sale. We have a Men of St. George Cooks group. We have brunches monthly. Coffee hour with sweet treats weekly. Thanksgiving dinners in our child care center, The Children's Ark. Chili cook offs. Chicken barbecues. Strawberry festivals. Progressive dinners. Youth group dinners. New member dinners. It seems we have worked food into almost every facet of our church life. We even serve refreshments at Vestry meetings!

So it seemed only natural to create a cookbook to capture this important part of our parish life and to share it with others who are not part of our worshiping family. While some of you may be asking, "Does the world need another cookbook?" we at St. George's have the audacity to present our third offering to this bountiful genre. We produced our first cookbook in the fifties, and then published a second edition in the eighties, and now, here we come again, completing our culinary trilogy in 2003.

Robert Farrar Capon, an Episcopal priest and author of the cookbook, '*The Supper of the Lamb*', instructs:

"To be sure, food keeps us alive, but that is only its smallest and temporary work. Its eternal purpose is to furnish our sensibilities against the day when we shall sit down at the heavenly banquet and see how gracious the Lord is. Nourishment is necessary only for a while; what we shall need forever is taste."

It is our hope that our little bound bundle of recipes will give you a taste of St. George's community and of our readiness to celebrate the goodness of the Creator. As the French say, "à table", come to the table. At St. George's you are always welcome.

Table of Measurements

This measurement	Equals this measurement
3 teaspoons	1 tablespoon
2 tablespoons liquid	1 ounce
6 tablespoons	3/8 cup
4 tablespoons	1/4 cup
5 1/3 tablespoons	1/3 cup
8 tablespoons	1/2 cup
16 tablespoons	1 cup
1 cup	8 ounces or 1/2 pint
2 cups	1 pint
4 cups	1 quart
2 pints	1 quart
4 quarts	1 gallon
8 quarts	1 peck
4 pecks	1 bushel
2 tablespoons fat or butter	1 ounce
1 stick butter	1/2 cup
1/2 pound butter or lard	1 cup
1 pound granulated sugar	2 cups
1 pound brown sugar	3 cups
1 pound confectioners' sugar	3 1/2 cups
1 pound flour	4 cups
1 pound rice	2 cups
1 square chocolate	1 ounce
16 marshmallows	1/4 pound
1 pound cornstarch	3 cups
1 pound diced cooked chicken	3 cups
1 pound cranberries	4 cups
1 pound chopped onions	3 cups
1 pound ground beef	2 cups
1 cup egg whites	8 to 12
1 cup egg yolks	13 to 14
1 cup whole eggs	5 eggs
1 cup lemon juice	4 to 6 lemons
1 pound bananas	3 medium
1 pound potatoes	3 to 4 medium
1 cup bread crumbs	2 3/4 ounces
1 pound shredded coconut	5 cups

Butter or margarine may be measured in the same way as solid shortening. If stick butter or margarine is used, measurements may be made by the following amounts:

1/4 stick equals 2 tablespoons
1/2 stick equals 4 tablespoons or 1/4 cup
1 stick equals 1/2 cup or 1/4 pound 4 sticks equal 2 cups or 1 pound

Substitutions Table

If you don't have this	You can use this
1 tablespoon cornstarch	2 tablespoons flour
1 cup pre-sifted flour	1 cup plus 2 tablespoons sifted cake flour
1 teaspoon baking powder	1 teaspoon cream of tartar plus 1 teaspoon baking soda
1 cup sour milk or buttermilk	1 cup sweet milk plus 1 tablespoon vinegar
1 square (1 ounce) chocolate	3 tablespoons cocoa powder plus 1 tablespoon shortening
⅔ cup honey	1 cup sugar plus ⅓ cup water
1 ½ cups corn syrup	1 cup sugar plus ½ cup water
1 whole egg	2 egg yolks plus 1 tablespoon water
1 cup tomatoes	1 ⅓ cup chopped fresh tomatoes simmered for 10 minutes
1 teaspoon oregano	1 teaspoon marjoram
½ cup catsup or chili sauce	½ cup tomato sauce plus 2 tablespoons sugar, 1 tablespoon vinegar, ⅛ teaspoon ground cloves
Few drops Tabasco	Dash of cayenne or red pepper
1 teaspoon Worcestershire	1 teaspoon bottled steak sauce
½ cup tartar sauce	6 tablespoons mayonnaise plus 2 tablespoons chopped pickle relish
1 cup tomato juice	½ cup tomato sauce plus ½ cup water
1 cup beef bouillon	1 beef bouillon cube or 1 envelope instant broth or 1 teaspoon beef extract dissolved in 1 cup boiling water
1 cup canned chicken broth	1 chicken bouillon cube or 1 envelope instant chicken broth dissolved in 1 cup boiling water
1 cup chicken or beef stock	1 cup canned chicken or beef broth
½ pound mushrooms	4 ounce can mushroom caps
3 ounce can Chinese noodles	2- 2¼ cans potato sticks
10 ounce package frozen strawberries	1 cup sliced fresh strawberries plus ⅓ cup sugar
½ cup raisins	½ cup dried prunes
1 pound shrimp, shelled, deveined and cooked	5 ounce can shrimp
½ pound ground pork	½ pound sausage meat
1½ cups diced cooked ham	12 ounce can pork luncheon meat, diced
1 teaspoon Italian seasoning	¼ teaspoon each oregano, basil, thyme and rosemary plus dash of cayenne
1 teaspoon pumpkin pie spice	½ teaspoon cinnamon, ¼ teaspoon ginger, ⅛ teaspoon each ground nutmeg and cloves
¼ cup cinnamon sugar	¼ cup granulated sugar plus 1 teaspoon cinnamon
1 teaspoon allspice	½ teaspoon cinnamon plus ⅛ teaspoon ground cloves

What Makes What

Before Preparation

Cereals and Pasta
1 cup quick-cooking oats
1 cup macaroni
1 cup noodles or spaghetti
1 cup rice
1 cup corn meal

Crackers and Bread
18 small crackers
21 small crackers
9 graham cracker squares
11 to 12 graham cracker squares
26 to 30 vanilla wafers
9 slices zwieback
1 slice bread
1 cup potato chips, firmly packed
12 thin pretzels

Dried Fruit
1 pound prunes (2$^3/_4$ cups)
1 pound apricots (3 to 3$^3/_4$ cups)
1 pound peaches (3$^2/_3$ cups)
1 pound figs (2$^1/_4$ cups)
1 pound pears (2$^2/_3$ cups)
1 pound raisins (3 to 3$^1/_4$ cups)
1 pound dates (2$^1/_2$ cups)

Fresh Fruits
1 pound apples (3 medium)
1 quart cherries
1 pound grapes
1 average lemon
1 average orange
1 pound cranberries (4$^3/_4$ cups)

Fresh Vegetables
1 pound beets (4 medium)
1 pound cabbage
1 pound carrots (7 to 8 medium)
1 pound celery (2 small bunches)
12 ears corn
1 pound potatoes

Cream, Cheese and Eggs
1 cup heavy cream
1 pound cheese
12 hard-cooked eggs

After Preparation

Cereals and Pasta
1$^3/_4$ cups cooked
2 cups cooked
2 cups cooked
3 cups cooked
4 cups cooked

Crackers and Bread
1 cup coarsely crushed
1 cup finely crushed
1 cup coarsely crumbled
1 cup finely crumbled
1 cup finely crumbled
1 cup finely crumbled
$^1/_2$ cup finely crumbed
$^1/_2$ cup potato chip crumbs
$^1/_2$ cup pretzel crumbs

Dried Fruit
4 cups cooked
4$^1/_2$ cups cooked
4$^1/_2$cups cooked
4$^1/_2$cups cooked
5$^1/_3$ cups cooked
4 cups cooked
1$^3/_4$ cups pitted

Fresh Fruits
3 cups pared and diced
2 cups pitted
2$^3/_4$ cups seeded
3 to 4 tbsp. juice and 1$^1/_2$ tsp. grated rind
$^1/_2$ cup juice ,1 cup diced pulp, 1 tbsp. grated rind
3 to 3$^1/_2$ cups sauce

Fresh Vegetables
2 cups diced
4 cups shredded
4 cups diced
4 cups diced
3 cups cut kernels
2$^1/_2$ cups diced

Cream, Cheese and Eggs
2 cups whipped
4 cups shredded
3$^1/_2$ cups chopped

Breads &
Brunches

APPLESAUCE RAISIN BREAD

A sweet bread, ideal for teas or midday snacks.

Yield: 1 large loaf or 4 small loves. Easy. May be frozen.

Ingredients
1 egg, slightly beaten
1 c. applesauce, preferably homemade
1/4 c. butter or margarine melted
1/2 c. sugar
1/4 c. firmly packed brown sugar
2 c. flour
2 tsp. baking powder
3/4 tsp. salt
1/2 tsp. baking soda
1/2 tsp. cinnamon
1 tsp. nutmeg
1/2 tsp. ginger
1/2 c. raisins
Pecans or walnuts are optional

Directions
In a bowl, combine eggs, applesauce, butter and sugars. Blend well. Stir in flour, baking powder, salt, soda and spices and stir until smooth. Stir in raisins and nuts. Bake in a well-greased loaf pan at 350 degrees about 1 hour. Cool before removing from pan.

Ruth Legnini

BANANA BREAD

A great recipe from one of my North Carolina college roommates. It is quick, easy and delicious.

Yield: 1 loaf.

Ingredients
1/2 c. shortening
1 c. sugar
2 eggs
1 1/2 c. flour
1 tsp. baking soda
3 bananas, mashed (the riper the better)

Directions

Preheat the oven to 350 degrees. Cream together the shortening and sugar in a large bowl. Next, sift together the flour and the baking soda and add it to the shortening/sugar mixture. Next add the eggs and stir. Finally add in the 3 mashed bananas and mix thoroughly.

Put into a loaf pan that has been greased and lined with wax paper. Bake in the 350 degree oven for approximately 1 hour. Test for doneness with a toothpick.

Karen Schloesser

BEST BISCUITS

A St. George's favorite from our old cookbook

Yield: approximately. 12 biscuits

Ingredients
3 c. flour
1/2 tsp. salt
4 tsp. baking powder
1 tsp. baking soda
8 tbsp. cold shortening
2 eggs
1 1/4 c. buttermilk

Directions

Cut dry ingredients with shortening to resemble coarse meal. Mix eggs and buttermilk, and add most of it to flour mixture to make a uniformly moist dough.

Turn out the dough on wax paper and sprinkle with flour on both sides. Roll out and cut with biscuit cutter. Wet tops with remaining milk mixture and bake in a 400 degree oven for 15 minutes.

Recipe is easy to cut in half for a small family.

Virgina Bracken

Helpful Hints

Bread straight from the freezer is excellent for French Toast. It doesn't get soggy

---

CARROT AND PINEAPPLE BREAD

Quick to make. Low fat and freezes well.

Yield: 1 loaf

Ingredients
1 1/2 c. flour
1 tsp. baking powder
1 tsp. baking soda
1 tsp. cinnamon
1/2 tsp. salt
1/4 c. oil
1/2 c. crushed pineapple and the juice
1 c. white sugar
2 beaten eggs
1 c. grated carrots
1/4 c. walnuts, chopped (optional)

Directions
Mix all the dry ingredients. Combine the oil and sugar, stirring to mix. Beat in eggs and then the crushed pineapple. Add the dry ingredients and beat until smooth. Fold in carrots and nuts. Pour into a greased 8 x 4 inch loaf pan. Heat the oven to 350 degrees or 325 degrees if using a glass dish. Bake for 50 - 60 minutes.

Kate Gibbons

CHARLESTON BREAKFAST SHRIMP

I first had shrimp and grits at one of the many fine restaurant in Charleston, S.C. It was memorable - a spicy shrimp gravy smothering creamy grits.

Yield: 2 servings. Can be doubled or tripled for a brunch.

Ingredients
1 c. peeled shrimp (1/2 lb.) (small - medium seem to work best)
2 tbsp. lemon juice (1/8 c.)
salt and cayenne pepper to taste
3 tbsp. bacon grease
1 small onion, finely chopped (1/4 c.)
1 green bell pepper, finely chopped (1/4 c.)
2 tbsp. unbleached all-purpose flour (1/8 c.)
3/4 to 1 c. hot water or stock (shrimp, chicken or vegetable)

Directions

In a bowl, combine the shrimp, lemon juice and salt and pepper. Then set aside (I sprinkle on enough cayenne so you can clearly see the red flakes). Heat the bacon grease in a skillet and sauté the onion and pepper until barely softened, about 6 minutes. Sprinkle the flour over the vegetables and stir constantly for about 2 minutes, until the flour begins to brown slightly.

Add shrimp and about 1/4 c. of stock, stirring constantly and turning the shrimp so they cook evenly. Cook for another 2 minutes or until the shrimp are uniformly cooked and the gravy is smooth, thinning with stock, if necessary. Spoon over cheesy grits or just plain creamy grits.

Note: Source for stone-ground grits is Nora Mill Granary, 7107 South Main Street, Helen, GA 30545, phone: 1-800-927-2375 or on the Internet at: www.noramill.com.

Eileen McKernan

CHEESY GRITS

The grits used here are stone-ground - a must for serious low-country cooks. I have not found a source in our area. I order mine from Nora Mill Granary, a mill I visited in the hills of Georgia.

Yield: 8- 12 servings

Ingredients
8 c. water
2 c. stone-ground grits
6 tbsp. butter
2 tsp. Kosher salt
1 qt cream, milk or half and half (choice of 1)
3 eggs, slightly beaten
3 c. cheddar cheese, grated
1 tsp. cayenne pepper

Directions
Place the water and butter in a large, heavy bottom pot and bring to a boil. Add the grits and salt and continue cooking at a slow simmer until most of the water is absorbed by the grits. Stir occasionally so that the grits do not stick to the bottom of the pan (about 10 minutes).

Add milk, cream or half-and-half - about a cup at a time and continue to cook until absorbed. Continue adding all of the liquid, a bit at a time until the quart has been used. Stir as needed.

This process should take approximately 45 minutes.

The grits should be creamy as this point. Place creamy grits in a buttered 3 1/2 qt. casserole dish. Add the eggs, cheddar cheese and cayenne pepper. Bake at 350 degrees for 1 hour or until set. Try serving this with the Charleston Breakfast Shrimp.

Eileen McKernan

CHOCOLATE BANANA MUFFINS

A Pillsbury bake-off winner.

Ingredients
1 pkg. banana bread mix (Pillsbury)
2 oz. unsweetened chocolate (melted)
1 c. buttermilk
1/3 c. oil (not Olive oil)
1- 6 oz. pkg.of chocolate chips
2 eggs, beaten
1 tbsp. sugar

Directions
Stir 3 tbsp. buttermilk into melted chocolate. Add 1 tbsp. oil, blend. Combine rest of ingredients. Place in greased muffin tins. Sprinkle with sugar. Bake at 400 for 18 - 20 minutes.

Helen Lungren

CHOCOLATE TEA BREAD

Ingredients
1/4 c. butter softened
2/3 c. sugar
1 egg
2 c. cake flour
1 tsp. baking soda
3/4 tsp. salt
1/3 c. Hershey cocoa
1 tsp. cinnamon
1 c. buttermilk
1 c. raisins
3/4 c. chopped walnuts

Directions

Cream butter and sugar. Add egg and beat well. Mix and sift flour, baking soda, salt, cocoa and cinnamon. Add to mixture alternately with the buttermilk. Stir in raisins and nuts. Turn into greased bread pan (9 x 5 x 2 3/4 inch). Bake at 350 degrees for one hour or until done. Cool on wire rack. Spread with cream cheese, if desired.

Helen Lungren

CRANBERRY BREAD

Easy, do ahead and can be frozen

Yield: 4 - 6 servings

Ingredients

1 egg
1 c. walnuts, chopped
1 c. sugar
2 c. sifted all-purpose flour
1/2 tsp. salt
1/2 tsp. baking soda
1 1/2 tsp. baking powder
1 tbsp. grated orange rind
3/4 c. fresh orange juice
2 tbsp. shortening
1 c. whole cranberries, chopped in the blender

Directions

Sift dry ingredients. Add rind, juice and shortening. Add egg. Mix well. Add walnuts and cranberries. Place in greased loaf pan (9 x 5 x 3 inch) and bake at 325 degrees for 1 hour. Cool, remove from the pan and serve.

Karen Schloesser

DUTCH BLUEBERRY CAKE

Easy to make and a treat for breakfast time.

Yield: 9 - 12 servings

Ingredients

Cake:
3/4 c. sugar
1/4 c. vegetable oil

1 egg
1/2 c. milk
2 c. flour
2 tsp. baking powder
1/2 tsp. salt
2 c. blueberries, well drained

Topping:
1/4 c. butter or margarine
1/2 c. granulated sugar
1/3 c. flour
1/2 tsp. cinnamon

Directions

Cake:

Cream together sugar, oil and egg until lemon-colored. Stir in milk. Sift together flour, baking powder and salt and stir into the creamed mixture. Gently fold in blueberries. Spread batter into a greased and floured 9 x 9 inch square baking pan. Sprinkle with topping. Bake 45 - 50 minutes at 375 degrees. Serve warm.

Topping:

Melt butter. Stir in sugar, flour and cinnamon. Crumble over the cake batter.

Mildred Burns

EGG CASSEROLE

This is great because you can make it the day before and heat it on the day you need it.

Yield: 4 servings

Ingredients

4 slices bread, broken into pieces
6 eggs
1 tsp. salt
1 tsp. dry mustard
1 lb. sausage, ham or bacon
1 c. grated cheese cheddar, Swiss or mozzarella
2 c. milk

Directions

Cover the bottom of a 9 x 13 inch pan with bread pieces. Set aside. Beat eggs, add salt, milk and mustard. Brown Sausage. Place sausage and egg mixture into pan. Refrigerate overnight or at least several hours. Bake at 350 degrees for 45 minutes.

Jennifer Robelo

EGGS FU YUNG

A breakfast treat from the old St. George's Cookbook

Yield: 4 servings

Ingredients
5 eggs, beaten
1 1/2 c. cooked, diced pork
1 small onion, minced
1 1/2 c. bean sprouts, rinsed and drained
1 c. sliced mushrooms
1/4 c. salad oil
1/4 c. soy sauce
2 tbsp cornstarch
2 c. chicken broth
1/2 c. water

Directions
Eggs:
In a large measuring cup, combine eggs, pork, onion, bean sprouts and mushrooms. In a large skillet, heat 2 tbsp. of the oil over medium-high heat. Pour egg mixture by 1/2 cupfuls into the pan. Cook until light brown on both sides. Use more oil as needed. Serve with sauce ladled over the eggs.

Sauce:
In a small saucepan, heat to boiling 2 cups chicken broth and 1/4 cup of soy sauce. Combine 2 tbsp. cornstarch and 1/2 c. water. Stir broth. Cook, stirring until thickened. Ladle over eggs and serve.

Cleo Coyle

FATHER BILL'S CORNELL BREAD

This recipe was originally developed at Cornell University for its health benefits. Flax seed not only has a wonderful taste but the "good" kind of oil that fights the buildup of arterial plaque. Everybody knows what bran does.

Yield: 1 loaf of bread

Ingredients
1 c. water
1/4 c. flax seed
1/4 c. bran

2 3/4 c. bread flour
2 tsp. bread machine yeast
2 - 3 tbsp. nonfat dry milk
1 tsp. salt
2 - 3 tbsp. margarine
1/2 - 2/3 c. honey

Measurements are not exact; increasing or decreasing them a bit will not harm the recipe and will let you find the flavor you like best.

Directions

Grind the flax seed for a few seconds just enough to break it up a little. An electric coffee grinder works well for this. The slight grind gives the bread a little crunchy texture; grinding it more turns the seeds into meal, which is okay for those who don't like little "specks" in their bread. Not grinding it at all makes it pretty crunchy.

Warm the honey briefly in the microwave oven so that it will pour easily.

Put all ingredients into the bread machine pan. I add them in the order listed, but it probably doesn't make any difference since the machine mixes them together right away. Set the indicator on the machine, and turn on.

Notes: Flax seed is available at any health food store and in most farmer's markets. In this area "The Head Nut" on Haverford Avenue. is a good inexpensive source. Bran is available in most supermarkets. Check the cereal and the baking aisles.

Regular flour and yeast can be used, but bread flour has a better gluten content for the bread and bread yeast is more predictable for use in bread machines than other yeasts. In short, bread flour and bread yeast makes the dough rise better. Any margarine will work: I use Shedd's spread because of its better cholesterol factors.

Father Bill Duffey

HOMEMADE GRANOLA

This is truly the best granola I have tasted. It has been a favorite at various brunches, including St. George's. Spoon on a dollop of orange yogurt.....WOW!

Yield: 1 large container

Ingredients

4 c. old-fashioned rolled oats
2 c. sweetened,shredded coconut
2 c. sliced almonds
3/4 c. vegetable oil (Canola)

1/2 c. good honey
1 1/2 c. small diced dried apricots
1 c. small diced dried figs
1 c. dried cherries
1 c. dried cranberries
1 c. roasted cashews

Directions

Preheat oven to 325 degrees. Toss the oats, coconut and almonds together in a large bowl. Whisk together the oil and honey in a small bowl. Pour liquids over the oat mixture and stir with a wooden spoon until all the oats and nuts are coated. Pour onto a 13 x 18 inch baking sheet. Bake for about 25 minutes, stirring occasionally with a spatula, until the mixture turns a nice even golden brown.

Remove from the oven and cool, stirring occasionally. Add the dried fruit and nut mixture. Use whatever mixture your family enjoys, but I think the apricots, cranberries and cherries help to make this really yummy. This will keep for a long period of time in an airtight container.

Eileen McKernan

IRISH SODA BREAD

Makes two rounds of soda bread

Ingredients

4 c. flour
1/4 c. sugar
1 tsp. salt
1 tbsp. baking powder
1 tsp. baking soda
1/2 c. butter
2 c. raisins
1 tbsp. caraway seed
1-1/3 c. buttermilk
1 egg

Directions

Heat oven to 375. Sift together flour, sugar, salt, baking powder, and baking soda. Stir in butter until it resembles corn meal. Stir in raisins and caraway. Combine buttermilk and egg. Mix and pour into flour mixture. Knead lightly until smooth and shape into two round loaves, about 6 inches in diameter. Place each in round cake pan sprinkled with flour. With sharp knife, make an "x" about 2 inches long by 1/4 inch deep in center.

Bake about one hour.

Eileen Kammerer

JOANIE'S LEMON CREAM SCONES

Serve these tender, light scones with butter, jam, or lemon curd and a "nice cup of tea"!

Yield: 12 scones

Ingredients
2 c. all-purpose flour
1/4 c. plus 2 tbsp. sugar
1 tbsp. baking powder
1/2 tsp. salt
1/4 c. chopped dried apricots (about 4 1/2 ounces)
1-1/4 c. whipping cream
1 tbsp. plus 1 tsp. grated lemon peel
3 tbsp. unsalted butter, melted

Directions
Preheat oven to 425 degrees. Mix flour, 1/4 cup sugar, baking powder and salt in large bowl. Stir in apricots and 1 tbsp. lemon peel. Add whipping cream and stir just until dough forms.

Turn dough out onto lightly floured surface. Knead gently just until dough holds together. Form dough into 10 inch diameter, 1/2 inch thick round. Cut into 12 wedges. Transfer wedges to large baking sheet, spacing evenly.

Combine remaining 2 tbsp. sugar and 2 tsp. lemon peel in small bowl. Brush scones with melted butter. Sprinkle with sugar mixture.

Bake scones until light golden brown, about 15 minutes. Transfer to rack and cool slightly. Serve scones warm or at room temperature. (Can be prepared 1 day ahead).

Cool completely, wrap in foil, and store at room temperature.

Eileen Kammerer

KUGELHOF

Yield: 10 - 12 servings

Ingredients
1- 13 3/4 oz. package hot roll mix
1/4 c. warm water
1/3 c. butter
1/3 c. sugar
1/4 tsp. mace

2 tsp. orange peel
1 tsp. grated lemon peel
2 eggs beaten
1/2 c. milk, scalded and cooled
1 c. walnuts
powdered sugar

Directions

Soften yeast from roll mix in warm water. Cream butter, sugar, mace and peels together. Beat in eggs. Add yeast, milk and flour from mix; beat until smooth. Cover and let rise in warm place until doubled (1 - 1 1/2 hours). Stir down.

Chop 1/4 c. walnuts fine; sprinkle into a well greased 9 inch bundt pan. Chop remaining walnuts coarsely and stir into dough.

Spoon into pan; let rise until doubled, about 30 minutes.

Bake in a 375 degree oven about 35 minutes.

Let stand 5 minutes; remove from pan and sprinkle with powdered sugar.

Nancy Dorey

LEMON CURD

In some parts of England, this is called lemon butter. It's a tasty spread for toast, muffins, and especially on scones. Try it on "Joanie's Lemon Cream Scones" (see opposite)

Yield: approximately fills a 12 oz. jam jar

Ingredients

3 eggs
1 c. sugar
1 large or 2 small lemons - juice & a little rind
1 tbsp. butter

Directions

Beat eggs; add sugar and lemon. Place in double boiler and stir until thickened (about 10 minutes). Remove from heat and add butter. Stir and cool. Store in refrigerator.

Eileen Kammerer

ORANGE YOGURT

Spoon over the homemade granola which is on page 10.

Yield: 4 - 6 servings

Ingredients
1 qt. plain low-fat yogurt
1/4 c. raisins
1/4 c. chopped walnuts
1 1/2 tsp. pure vanilla extract
1/4 c. good honey
1 orange, grated zest of
1/2 - 1 c. freshly squeezed orange juice
orange, orange zest, raisins or walnuts (optional toppings)

Directions
Line a sieve with cheesecloth or paper towels and suspend it over a bowl. Pour yogurt into the sieve and allow it to drain. Refrigerate overnight.

Place thickened yogurt into a medium bowl and add the remaining ingredients. When serving with the granola, I omit the raisins and walnuts. Thin with orange juice to consistency desired. Use any of the toppings as a garnish.

Eileen McKernan

OVEN OMELET BRUNCH

Breakfast from the previous St. George's Cookbook

Yield: 10 - 12 servings

Ingredients
1/4 c. butter or margarine
1 1/2 dozen eggs
1 c. sour cream
1 c. milk
2 tsp. salt
1/4 c. chives, chopped

Directions
Heat oven to 325 degrees. Melt butter in a 13 x 9 inch pan in the oven. Beat eggs, sour cream, milk and salt until blended. Sprinkle on chives. Bake until set but still moist, about 35 minutes. Cheddar cheese may be substituted for, or added along with, the chives.

PUMPKIN MUFFINS

From the old Stouffer restaurants.

Ingredients
1 1/2 c. flour
2 tsp. baking powder
1 1/2 tsp. salt
1/2 c. sugar
1/2 tsp. cinnamon
1/2 tsp. nutmeg
1 egg
1/2 c. milk
1/2 c. canned pumpkin
1/4 c. butter melted
3/4 c. raisins

Directions
Combine dry ingredients (sift). Beat egg, add milk, mix thoroughly: add pumpkin and butter. Blend. Add liquid to dry ingredients and mix until moist. Add raisins and stir. Spoon batter into greased muffin tins. Sprinkle 1/4 tsp. sugar over each muffin. Bake at 400 for 18 - 20 minutes. Serve warm.

Helen Lungren

PUMPKIN NUT BREAD

A fall or really an any time treat for all.

Yield: 2 loaves or 36- 1/2 in. slices.

Ingredients
3 1/2 c. unsifted flour
2 tsp. baking soda
1 tsp. cinnamon
1 tsp. salt
1/2 tsp. double acting baking powder
1/2 tsp. ground allspice
2 2/3 c. sugar
1 c. salad oil
4 eggs
1/3 c. water
1 can (16oz.) pumpkin
1/2 c. walnuts or pecans, chopped

Directions

Preheat oven to 350 degrees. Grease 2- 9 x 5 x 2 3/4 inch loaf pans and set aside. Combine flour and next 5 ingredients and set aside. In a large mixing bowl, beat sugar and oil. Add eggs, water and pumpkin, beating well. Gradually add dry ingredients and stir just until blended. Stir in nuts. Pour batter into greased loaf pans. Bake for 55 - 60 minutes, until toothpick inserted in center comes out clean.

Remove from oven to wire rack. Cool 10 minutes, before removing from pans. Let cool completely on wire rack.

Mildred Burns

QUICHE LORRAINE WITH GRUYERE CHEESE AND BACON

Enjoyed at St. George's brunches. You can use other combinations such as spinach/feta, sun-dried tomatoes, broccoli, cheddar, mushrooms or bacon, mushroom and Swiss cheese.

Yield: 1- 11 inch Quiche

Ingredients
Crust:
1 1/2 c. flour
pinch of sugar
1/2 tsp. salt
5 1/2 tbsp. butter
3 tbsp. Crisco
1/4 c. ice water

Filling:
1 large sweet onion, sliced
3 small shallots, chopped
6 slices of bacon, fried until crisp
1 large chunk of Gruyere cheese, grated
1 1/2 c. heavy cream
4 eggs
salt, pepper, nutmeg
Dijon mustard

Directions
Crust:
Sift together the flour, sugar and salt. Add butter and Crisco to the sifted ingredients. Cut in with a pastry knife. Add ice water, a bit at a time until pastry comes together.

Form into a disk, wrap in plastic and refrigerate for about 30 minutes. Roll out dough and fit into quiche pan. Bake at 375 degrees for 25 minutes.

Filling:
Sauté the onion and shallots in butter over medium heat. Fry the bacon until it is crisp. Remove partially baked crust from the oven. Brush the bottom and sides with Dijon mustard to seal. Spread the onion and shallot mixture in the bottom. Next, spread the bacon on the top of the onion mixture. Then spread the cheese, saving a bit for the top. Whisk cream, eggs, salt, pepper, nutmeg together and pour over top. Sprinkle remaining cheese when the custard is partially set.

Bake at 325 degrees for 30 minutes or until set.

Eileen McKernan

RHUBARB BREAD

When rhubarb is in season, try this recipe.

Yield: 2- 9 x 5 x 2 3/4 inch loaves or 4- 6 x 3 x 2 inch loaves

Ingredients
1 1/2 c. brown sugar
2 3/4 c. flour
1 tsp. baking soda
1 egg
1 c. buttermilk
1/2 c. vegetable oil
1 tsp. vanilla
1 c. finely chopped rhubarb
2 tbsp. flour
butter
sugar

Directions
Grease 4- 6 x 3 x 2 inch pans or 2- 9 x 5 x 2 3/4 inch pans. Preheat oven to 350 degrees. In a large mixing bowl, stir together flour, brown sugar, baking soda and salt; set aside. In a mixing bowl, combine egg, buttermilk, oil and vanilla. Stir into dry ingredients, mixing well. Toss rhubarb with 2 tbsp. flour and fold into batter. Pour batter into prepared pans. Dot each loaf with 3 tsp. butter and sprinkle each loaf with 3 tsp. granulated sugar. Bake at 350 degrees for 40 minutes for the small loaves and 55 minutes for the large loaves until a toothpick inserted near the center comes out clean. Cool pans for 10 minutes. Remove from pans; cool thoroughly on wire rack. Serve warm or cool.

Mildred Burns

RHUBARB GLOOP

Fruit to put on top of your cereal.

Yield: 8 servings

Ingredients
3 medium, 2 thick or 4 slim stalks of rhubarb
1 pkg. (pint) of fresh strawberries cut up a bit
1/2 c. sugar
1/2 tsp. ground nutmeg
1/4 c. water

Directions
In a 3 qt. saucepan pour 1/4 c. water. Add the rhubarb cut into 1 inch squares, then the cut up strawberries and the sugar and nutmeg. Bring to a boil, stir it, turn heat down to medium or lower and cook, stirring often for about 15 minutes, until the fruit is broken down and has become gloop. Pour into a bowl and let it cool. Refrigerate. At breakfast give yourself about 1 big dessert spoonful on top of your cereal.

Cecily Littleton

TRADITIONAL WELSH CAKES

Recipe was dictated by my Welsh grandmother. We traditionally make the for St. David's Day - March 1st

Ingredients
4 c. flour
2 tsp. baking powder
1/2 tsp. salt
2 tsp. nutmeg
1 c. currants (or raisins)
1 1/2 c. sugar
1 1/2 c. shortening
2 eggs

Directions
Mix like pie crust. Roll to desired thickness (about 1/4 inch) cut with round cutter or floured glass, lip of desired size. Bake on a griddle or iron frying pan (like pancakes) till brown on both sides. Cool and store in a tightly covered metal or plastic container. They will keep for several weeks.

Dolores (Lewellyn Jones) Jaquith

ZUCCHINI BREAD

A versatile bread recipe.

Yield: 2- 5 x 9 inch loaves

Ingredients
4 c. flour
2 tsp. baking soda
1/4 tsp. baking powder
2 tsp. vanilla
3 eggs
1 c. oil
2 tbsp. molasses
2 - 3 c. grated zucchini
2 c. brown sugar
1 tsp. salt
2 tsp. cinnamon
raisins or nuts, optional

Directions
Preheat oven to 350 degrees. Grease 2- 5 x 9 inch loaf pans and set them aside.

Beat eggs, add oil, sugar, molasses and vanilla. Add dry ingredients. Add zucchini and raisins and nuts, if desired. Bake for 1 hour. or until done in a 350 degree oven.

Note: pumpkin can be substituted for zucchini in the recipe. If making pumpkin bread, substitute 2/3 c. milk for the oil and 2 - 2 1/2 c. pumpkin for the zucchini.

Mildred Burns

ZUCCHINI BREAD

Easy. May be frozen

Yield: 2 loaves or 8 small.

Ingredients
4 extra large eggs
2 c. sugar
1 c. oil (a little less)
3 1/2 c. flour
1 1/4 tsp. baking soda
1/2 tsp. baking powder

1 1/2 tsp. salt
1 tsp. allspice
1 tsp. cinnamon
1/4 tsp. nutmeg
4 c. grated zucchini
1 c. broken walnuts
1 c. dark raisins
1 tsp. vanilla

Directions

Whisk eggs and sugar in large bowl until lemon colored. Mix in oil. Sift dry ingredients and blend a little into egg mixture. Add 2 c. zucchini then remaining dry ingredients. Mix in remaining zucchini. Add walnuts, raisins and vanilla.

Bake in 2 greased, sugared loaf pans at 350 degrees for 50 - 60 minutes. Less time for small.

Ruth Legnini

Appetizers &
Hors d'Oeuvres

ASPARAGUS WRAPPED IN PROSCIUTTO

An easy, elegant, make-ahead appetizer that can be doubled or tripled for large crowds.

Yield: 24 pieces.

Ingredients
2 lbs. fresh asparagus, cleaned and tough ends discarded (approx. 24 spears)
6 oz. Boursin cheese
2 tbsp. sour cream
1/4 to 1/2 lb. prosciutto, sliced very thin

Directions
Blanch the asparagus in boiling salted water until tender crisp and then plunge in an ice-water bath. Mix the Boursin and sour cream until you get a smooth consistency.

Lay out the sheets of prosciutto and place a small amount of the cheese mixture in a line in the center of the slice from left to right. Put one asparagus spear (if large or 2 - 3 spears if small) topped with prosciutto and roll it up.

Refrigerate 1 - 4 hours keeping covered. Serve chilled or at room temperature.

Note: the asparagus should still be crunchy and needs only 1 - 2 minutes in the boiling water. The ice bath prevents further cooking.

It's your choice about the size of the spears. I prefer small but the important thing is that they not be overcooked.

Terri McFarland

BACON AND WATER CHESTNUT ROLL-UPS

Always a Smythe staple at our Christmas party. They taste like candy.

Yield: 15 - 18. Must do part of this recipe ahead of time.

Ingredients
1- 8 oz. can of whole water chestnuts
1/4 to 1/3 c. soy sauce
brown sugar
1/2 lb. bacon

Directions

If the water chestnuts are large then cut them in half. Marinate the water chestnuts in soy sauce for several hours or even overnight.

Roll each chestnut in brown sugar and then wrap it in 1/2 slice of bacon. Fasten it with a toothpick. Place on a cookie sheet which has sides. May be done ahead to this point.

Bake at 200 degrees for 1 hour until the bacon is well done. Do this the morning of the day you want to serve them. Then place them in the microwave to heat them up.

Bryn Smythe

CARAMELIZED ONION AND ROASTED RED PEPPER PIZZA

A neat hors d'oeuvre to serve at a party.

Yield: approximately 20 servings.

Ingredients
1 tbsp. olive oil
2 large onions, cut in half and thinly sliced
1/2 tsp. salt
1 jar (12 oz.) roasted red peppers, drained, patted dry and chopped coarsely
2 tbsp. balsamic vinegar
5 whole wheat pitas or flat breads (8 inches each)
1/3 c. (1 1/2 oz.) freshly shaved Parmesan cheese (or soy alternative)
1/4 c. (loosely packed) fresh basil, cut into strips

Directions
Preheat the oven to 400 degrees. Heat the oil in a large non-stick skillet over medium heat. Add the onions and salt and cook for 20 minutes, stirring occasionally, until the onions are quite tender and golden brown. Stir in the peppers and vinegar.

Place the pitas or flat breads on a baking sheet. Divide the onion mixture evenly over the pitas and sprinkle with the shaved Parmesan.

Bake until the pitas are crisp, about 10 minutes. Remove the pizzas from the oven and sprinkle with the basil.

To serve, cut each pizza into quarters.

Terry McFarland

CHEDDAR BEER SPREAD

A wonderful party treat.

Yield: 6 - 8 servings.

Ingredients
1/2 lb. (8 oz.) shredded sharp cheddar
1 crushed clove garlic
dash cayenne pepper or Tabasco
1 tbsp. Worcestershire sauce
1/2 tsp. dry mustard
1/4 c. beer

Directions
Combine and mix all ingredients until very smooth (a food processor is the easiest way to do this.) Fill a low crock or cup or bowl. Keep in the refrigerator (can keep at least a month).

Remove from refrigerator and let it come to room temperature. Serve with crackers.

Jennifer Robelo

CHICKEN NIPS

Kids love this too instead of Chix nuggets. I make 4 times the recipe for larger groups.

Yield: 60 pieces. Can be prepared ahead and frozen.

Ingredients
4 whole boneless chicken breasts
1/2 c. melted butter

Crispy Coating:
1 c. crushed champagne crackers
1/2 c. grated parmesan cheese
1/4 c. finely chopped walnuts
1 tsp. dried thyme
1 tsp. dried basil
1/2 tsp. salt
1/4 tsp. pepper

Zesty Dip:
1/2 c. Dijon mustard
1/4 c. sour cream

Directions

Cut chicken into long bite-sized pieces. Dip each piece into melted butter. Combine the Crispy Coating ingredients. Roll each chicken piece in the coating and place the pieces on foil-lined baking sheets.

Bake for 20 minutes at 400 degrees.

For a great dipping sauce, combine the mustard and sour cream.

Bryn Smythe

CHILI CON QUESCO PIE

This recipe can be made more or less spicy...we like it HOT!

Yield: One pie makes 6 servings

Ingredients

4 eggs, beaten
1 can (4oz.) green chilies (we used sliced jalapenos)
12 oz. Monterey Jack cheese, sliced thin or shredded

Directions

Preheat oven to 300 degrees. Lightly grease a 9 inch pie plate (preferably one that can be used to serve from) or baking dish. Drain chilies: cut so that they will lie flat. Line prepared pan with chilies. Cover with cheese.

Pour beaten eggs over the top.

Bake at 300 degrees for 50 - 60 minutes, until set.

Terry McFarland

Helpful Hints

Remove pimento from green olives and stuff with blue cheese.

CLAMS ON THE GRILL

Yield: 50 - 100 clams.

Ingredients

50 - 100 clams
4 1/2 oz. jar of chopped garlic
12 - 14 oz. can of diced tomatoes
1 medium onion, sliced
7 oz. jar of roasted peppers
1/2 c. shopped parsley
1/2 c. chopped cilantro
3 - 4 sliced jalapeno peppers
1 can or bottle of beer
salt and pepper to taste

Directions

Clean the clams. If you put them into water with ice and sprinkle flour or baking soda over them, they will spit out any sand that is in them. Put the clams in a 9 x 13 x 2 inch aluminum pan, add all the ingredients with their juices. Cover with foil and place on a hot grill. Serve when all the clams are open.

Liz Havens

CRAB DIP

Everyone loves this crab dip!

Yield: 8 - 10 servings.

Ingredients

1- 8 oz. can of crab meat
1- 8 oz. pkg. cream cheese
1 pkg. of dried Italian salad dressing mix
2 - 3 tbsp. mayonnaise
Old Bay Seasonings or cayenne pepper
1 or 2 tbsp. dry parsley
club crackers

Directions

Drain the crab meat and mix it together with the cream cheese. Add the Italian dressing mix and the mayonnaise and mix thoroughly. Add the Old Bay Seasoning and parsley and mix again.

Chill the entire mixture for 30 minutes. Then serve with crackers.

Eric Hartline

CRANBERRY DELIGHT

Serve this appetizer with crackers.

Yield: 3 cups.

Ingredients
1- 12 oz. pkg. of cream cheese
1 c. water
1 c. sugar
1 pkg. (12 oz.) cranberries (fresh or frozen)
1/2 c. apricot preserves
2 tbsp. lemon juice
1/3 c. slivered almonds, toasted

Directions
Over a medium heat, bring water and sugar to a boil without stirring for 5 minutes. Add cranberries and cook until they pop.

Remove from heat and stir in apricot preserves and lemon juice. Cool.

Add almonds, stir and spoon over cream cheese. Store leftovers in the refrigerator.

Helen Lungren

CURRIED CHICKEN BALLS

Lessen the preparation time by cooking the chicken a day ahead. These will easily freeze and keep for up to 6 weeks

Yield: 50 pieces

Ingredients
1 1/2 lb. boneless chicken
8 oz. pkg. cream cheese
4 tbsp. mayonnaise
1 1/2 tbsp. chopped almonds, sautéed in 1 tbsp. butter
3 tbsp. chopped chutney
1 tsp. salt
3 tsp. curry powder, or to taste
1 c. grated coconut to cover
2 tbsp. butter or margarine

Directions

Melt margarine or butter and sauté chicken, or bake in a 350 degree oven. Do not over-cook. Chill before proceeding with the recipe.

Chop chicken finely in a food processor, grind or chop finely. Measure out 2 cups of the chicken and place in a large bowl. Mix in and blend well all other ingredients except the coconut.

Place in the refrigerator until contents are cold and stiff in order to shape the balls more easily. Form 1 inch balls with the mixture, either by hand or using a cookie dough dispenser will help.

Put coconut in a gallon size plastic bag. Place 6 - 7 balls in at a time and shake gently to cover. Place balls on a flat tray in one layer. Place in refrigerator until chilled and then pack in a container using wax paper to separate layers. Freeze if not using by the next day.

To freeze: line a cookie sheet with wax paper, place balls in a single layer, sides not touching. Cover with another sheet of wax paper. Freeze until hard and then pack in a container as above.

Kate Gibbons

FRESH MEXICAN SALSA

My first experience with fresh salsa was in a restaurant in Oxnard, CA. After several experiments, this is my favorite.

Yield: 6 - 8 servings

Ingredients
4 over ripe large tomatoes, seeded
1 fresh jalapeno pepper, seeded
1 medium onion
1 clove garlic
10 sprigs fresh cilantro
1/2 tsp. salt
juice of a fresh squeezed lime

Directions
Put everything except tomatoes in a food processor and chop fine.

Add tomatoes but chop course - approx. 1/4 inch chunks. Refrigerate for 2 hours.

This will last over 1 week in the fridge.

Notes: If seeds of jalapeno are included the mix will be much hotter! Make a double batch for a large party with 3 seeded jalapenos. The fresh Italian plum tomatoes also work and are more available in markets during winter.

Don DiPaulo

GOAT CHEESE AND PESTO TORTE

A nice colorful presentation which is beautiful for Christmas. I serve it every year.

Yield: 16 servings. Serve with bland crackers.

Ingredients
8 oz. cream cheese, softened
12 oz. Montrachet goat cheese
1 c. butter, softened
1 c. basil pesto
1 c. drained, minced sun-dried tomatoes

Directions
Combine cheeses and butter in bowl. Beat well until the mixture is blended and fluffy.

Line an 8 inch cake pan with dampened cheesecloth while leaving enough cloth on the sides to cover the top later. Layer 1/3 of the cheese mixture, 1/2 of the pesto, 1/3 of the cheese mixture, remaining pesto and remaining cheese mixture into the cake pan. Cover with plastic wrap and fold the cheesecloth over the top.

Chill for 1 hour or up to 3 days.

Fold back the cheesecloth from the top of the torte and remove the plastic wrap. Invert the torte on a serving plate: remove the cheesecloth. Top with sun-dried tomatoes.

Bryn Smythe

Helpful Hints

Roll cream cheese balls in minced chipped beef

GUACAMOLE DIP

A real hit at garden parties, cocktail parties or any party.

Yield: 6 - 8 servings
Serve with taco chips. This may be made one day ahead and refrigerated. Remove from the refrigerator one hour before serving.

Ingredients
2 cans of Frito Lay jalapeno dip
2 ripe avocados, mashed
2 tbsp. lemon juice
1/2 tsp. salt
1/2 tsp. pepper
8 oz. sour cream
1/2 c. mayonnaise
1 pkg. taco seasoning
2 tomatoes, chopped
1 bunch scallions
1 - 2 c. grated cheddar cheese

Directions
Layer the following ingredients, in the order listed, in a quiche dish.
2 cans jalapeno dip
2 ripe avocados, mashed with: lemon juice, salt and pepper
Sour cream mixed with: mayonnaise and taco seasoning
2 tomatoes, chopped
Scallions, chopped
Grated cheddar cheese

Mary Geisz

HAM PINWHEELS

A very quick and easy appetizer for someone in a hurry.

Ingredients
1 1/2 lb. ham (sliced in package)
1 lb. cream cheese
1 jar pickles (long slices)

Directions
Lay out a ham slice. Spread with softened cream cheese. Place slice of pickle at one end. Roll, refrigerate, then cut into 1/2" slices.

Loretta Beckey

MEXICAN DIP

A great Mexican dip to use with tortilla chips. A recipe from St. George's Cookbook.

Yield: 6 - 8 servings

Ingredients
8 oz. cream cheese
1 can black bean soup
2 tbsp. grated onion
Tabasco
dash of garlic powder

Directions
Mix in blender: the cream cheese, black bean soup, grated onion, dash of Tabasco and a dash of garlic powder.

Mary Beumer

MOCK PATE

A quick and festive hors d'oeuvre.

Yield: enough for a small party
Serve with small party rye bread.

Ingredients
8 oz. liverwurst
8 oz. cream cheese
2 tbsp. dry onion soup mix
2 tsp. lemon juice
1 tbsp. Worcestershire sauce
parsley flakes

Directions
Cream all ingredients together in a large bowl. Form mixture into a ball. Cover the ball in parsley flakes. It is helpful to sprinkle the parsley flakes onto tin foil and then roll the ball over them to cover it on all sides.

If you make this ahead then wrap in foil and place in the refrigerator so the pate will set.

Karen Schloesser

OYSTERS ROCKEFELLER

Here is another blast from the past St. George's Cookbook .

Yield: 6 servings.

Ingredients
36 oysters
2 c. spinach (or watercress), chopped
1/4 c. minced onion
1 bay leaf
1 tbsp. minced parsley
1/2 tsp. salt
1/2 tsp. celery salt
6 drops red hot pepper sauce
6 tbsp. butter
1/2 c. bread crumbs
lemon wedges for garnish

Directions
Drain oysters. Place them on a buttered baking dish. Put greens, onion, bay leaf and parsley through food grinder. Add salt, celery salt and pepper sauce. Cook mixture in butter for 5 minutes. Add bread crumbs to mixture and mix well. Spread mixture over oysters. Bake in preheated 400 degree oven for 10 minutes or until edges of oysters begin to curl. When possible, I like to put the mixture on the oysters in the half shell.

Helene Keller

PORK SAUSAGE ROLLS

Popular British Christmas fare. Often eaten whilst gifts are opened or as an appetizer.

Yield: Approximately 30- 2 inch rolls

Ingredients
1 box Pepperidge Farm puff pastry sheets
1 1lb. tube of Bob Evans ground pork
1 egg beaten with 1 tbsp. milk
flour for dusting rolling pin and board
cold water
1 small basting brush
1 small sharp knife
1 or 2 ungreased flat cookie sheets

Directions

Defrost the pastry as instructed. Use one sheet at a time. Roll the pastry out to 1/8 inch thickness. Cut the sheet in half across the width and work with one half at a time. Lightly flour hands and form a roll with the sausage about 1 inch in diameter and the length of the bottom edge of the pastry.

Place the sausage roll along the bottom edge of the pastry, leaving a 1/4 inch border. Lift pastry and sausage up to encircle in the pastry, leaving an edge to seal with the bottom edge. Brush the edges with water and seal them together. Cut the roll into 2 inch long rolls (the end of the rolls will be open).

Make 2 diagonal slashes through the top of each pastry on each roll. Brush tops of the rolls with the beaten egg. Place rolls seam side down on a cookie sheet an inch apart. Repeat with other pastry half.

Place rack in middle of the oven and heat to 425 degrees. Cook the rolls for 25 - 30 minutes until the pastry is risen and brown. Note: using the 2 sheets of pastry in the box and 1- 1 lb. roll of ground pork will make about 30- 2 inch rolls.

Kate Gibbons

RITA'S (NO) ROASTED PEPPERS

This recipe came from Rita Cooper. She gave it to me many years ago and I have used it many times. It works as an appetizer on Italian bread, as an accompaniment for sandwiches or on a buffet table. It's a great way to roast peppers without the mess.

All ingredients can be adjusted to taste.

Yield: 8 - 10 servings

Ingredients
3 tbsp. olive oil
6 peppers, sliced, mostly red but can use yellow and green for color
2 small onions, chopped
2 cloves garlic finely chopped
salt and pepper to taste
few hot pepper flakes (optional)
1 sprig fresh basil
1 sprig fresh oregano (may use a dash or 2 of dried)
juice of one lemon
1 tsp. red wine vinegar
several sprigs of fresh parsley
black olives (optional for garnish)

Directions

Sauté chopped onions and garlic in olive oil until caramelized. Add salt, pepper, hot pepper flakes, oregano and basil. Add sliced peppers and continue sautéing. The peppers will be soft and browned when finished. Remove from heat and add vinegar, lemon juice and chopped parsley. Correct seasonings and garnish with black olives.

Donna DiPaulo

SAUSAGE PINWHEELS

An easy and quick recipe

Yield: 12 servings

Ingredients
1 tube (8 oz.) Crescent rolls
1/2 lb. uncooked sausage
2 tbsp. minced chives

Directions

Unroll the Crescent roll dough on a lightly floured surface. Press the seams together. Roll into a 14 x 10 inch rectangle. Spread sausage to within 1/2 inch of the edge. Sprinkle with chives. Roll up from the long side and cut into 12 slices.

Bake 1 inch apart on an ungreased baking sheet in a 375 degree oven for 12 - 16 minutes or until golden brown.

Helen Lungren

STUFFED DIPPING BREAD

A festive presentation for a party.

Yield: 6 - 8 servings

Ingredients
1 round loaf of bread
2 onions, sliced
1 leek
olive oil
18 oz. mayonnaise
1 bag of bacon bits
8 oz. parmesan cheese, grated
sliced baguette for dipping

Directions

Cut a hole in the bread and empty all of the interior, leaving a bowl-shaped bread. Slice the onions in half rings. Chop the leek and sauté it and the onions with very little olive oil. Then place the sautéed mix in a bowl and add the bacon bits, mayo and cheese.

Mix everything and put it in the bread and place in the oven for 45 minutes to 1 hour at 350 degrees. Check every 5 minutes. In order to get the bread a little crunchy, you can increase the temperature a bit at the end.

If you are under a time constraint, you can microwave the mix for 3 minutes while it is still in the bowl and then place it in the bread. After that, place in the oven at 375 degrees until the bread gets crunchy.

Place the bread on a plate and slice a baguette to dip in the mix.

Francisco Robelo

STUFFED MUSHROOMS

They made their first appearance at St. George's during the 2002 "Men of St. George's Cook Event". Great as an appetizer or exclude the caps and use it for your Thanksgiving turkey stuffing.

Yield: 60 servings

Ingredients
Approx. 60 small to medium mushrooms
1/2 stick of butter
2 medium onions, chopped
2 pks. Jimmy Dean's Sausage
3/4 c. water
Italian bread crumbs

Directions

Saute onions in butter. Remove mushroom stems from caps and finely chop the stems (a food processor works great). Add chopped stems to onions and saute additional 5-10 minutes.

Break up sausage and add in, cool for a few minutes.

Add water, bring to a boil and fully cook sausage. Add Italian bread crumbs until it is the consistency of dressing. Lower heat, mix around and let cool .

Fill mushroom caps and bake at 350 degrees for 15 - 20 minutes or until bubbly.

Tim Wagner

TOASTY ONION STICKS

This recipe freezes well.

Yield: 96 sticks

Ingredients
24 slices of very thin white bread (Pepperidge Farm, or similar)
1 envelope Lipton onion soup mix
1/2 lb. butter or margarine

Directions
Mix softened butter or margarine and Lipton onion soup mix. Trim the crusts from the bread and spread slices with the onion butter. Cut each slice of bread into 4 strips. Place on ungreased baking sheet. Bake for 10 minutes at 375 degrees.

Stephanie Mahoney

Helpful Hints

Serve dips in hollowed out peppers, artichokes or red cabbage. Remove thin slice from the bottom so it will stand up.

A quick dip: ½ pt. sour cream and 1 pkg. Hidden Valley Ranch Salad dressing.

Soups &
Sauces

CHICKEN GUMBO SOUP

Yield: 4 to 6 servings

Ingredients

2 c. cooked chicken
2 tbsp. butter
2 tbsp. oil (not olive oil)
1 onion chopped
1 clove garlic chopped
1- 14 1/2 oz. can stewed tomatoes
1/2 c. chopped green pepper
1 c. frozen okra, sliced
3 tbsp. uncooked rice (not "minute rice")
3- 14 1/2 oz. cans chicken broth
1 tsp. salt
1 tsp. pepper
1/4 tsp. tarragon
1 tsp. Tabasco sauce
1 bay leaf

Directions

Mix all ingredients, except chicken, in large soup pot. Bring to a boil. Cover and simmer about 25 minutes. Add chicken, cook about 10 minutes longer. Remove bay leaf.

Helen Lungren

CORN CHOWDER

Excellent on a cold winter's day

Yield: 4 servings

Ingredients

5 slices bacon
1 medium onion
2 c. whole kernel corn
1 c. diced canned potatoes
1 can mushroom soup
2 1/2 c. milk
1 tsp. salt
dash of pepper
butter

Directions
Cook bacon in a large pot and reserve the drippings. Remove the bacon and cook the onion in the bacon drippings. Add remaining ingredients.

Heat to boiling; reduce heat and simmer until heated through. Dot with butter - 1 for each serving.

Karen Schloesser

CREAMY DILL POTATO SOUP

This is a wonderfully rich and creamy soup - enjoyed during Lenten suppers and Lenten Quiet Day. While meatless, it is certainly flavorful and delicious.

Yield: 6 - 8 servings as a first course / 4 servings as a main course

Ingredients
7 Idaho Potatoes, peeled and cubed
2 onions, chopped
1 pint heavy cream
½ stick butter
1 c. sour cream
bunch of chopped green onions
bunch of chopped fresh dill
Kosher salt / freshly ground pepper / crumbled bacon (optional) / more sour cream

Directions
Using a large, heavy bottom pot, cook the potatoes and onions in enough water to cover until potatoes begin to fall apart. Drain, return to the pot. Add cream, butter, sour cream, green onions and dill. Stir to incorporate

Cook for 10 minutes over adjusted heat so as not to scorch. Add salt, pepper and bacon. Adjust seasonings and sour cream to taste - should be rich, creamy, and yummy. May or may not add bacon, more chopped dill etc.

ENJOY !

Eileen McKernan

Helpful Hints
Fine dry bread crumbs make a good thickener for cream sauces in casseroles.
Use them whenever you want a toasted flavor in sauce

CURRIED SPLIT PEA SOUP

This is especially good in the winter. Makes a meal with salad and rolls.

Yield: 6 - 8 servings

Ingredients
2 c. dried split peas
3 cans chicken broth
1 large carrot, grated
2 medium potatoes, grated
1 large onion, finely chopped
1 tsp. curry powder
1/2 tsp. salt
1/4 tsp. pepper
1 c. cooked rice

Directions
Presoak and wash peas. Drain and place in large pot with tight fitting lid. Add chicken broth, carrot, potatoes, onion, curry powder, salt and pepper. Cover and bring to boil. Simmer about 2 hours or until peas are soft.

Check and add water as needed. Add rice and serve.

Mary Lou Toal

GAZPACHO

A wonderful cold summer soup

Yield: 4 servings

Ingredients
1 cup finely chopped, peeled tomato (Hint: dip the tomato in boiling water pull it out and the skin will peel off easily)
1/2 c. each finely chopped green pepper, celery and cucumber
1/4 c. onion, chopped
2 tsp. parsley
1 tsp. chives
1 clove minced garlic
2 - 3 tbsp tarragon wine vinegar
2 tbsp. olive oil
1 tsp. salt
1/4 tsp. black pepper

1/2 tsp. Worcestershire sauce
2 c. tomato juice

Directions
Combine all of the ingredients in a stainless steel or glass bowl. Cover and chill for 4 hours. Serve with croutons.

Karen Schloesser

MARIANNE'S GAZPACHO

A refreshing soup for summer.

Yield: 6 - 8 servings

Ingredients
1 large can whole Italian style tomatoes with juice
2 cucumbers, peeled, seeded, chopped
2 green peppers, seeded, chopped
1 large onion, peeled, chopped
2 carrots, peeled, chopped (optional - cuts acidity a little)
2 cloves garlic, peeled, chopped *
3 ribs celery, chopped*
4 scallions, chopped*
1 tbsp. lime juice
1 tbsp. hot sauce*
1/4 c. extra virgin olive oil
sea salt and fresh black pepper to taste
1/4 to 1/2 c. fresh chopped cilantro (optional)
scallion greens for garnish
*more or less to taste on these ingredients

Directions
Individually whiz the first 8 ingredients in food processor to a fine consistency. Combine in a large bowl with next 5 ingredients. Cover the bowl tightly and allow the flavors to combine for at least several hours - overnight is best.

It might be necessary to add additional liquid as the gazpacho sets - water or tomato juice will work fine. Serve cold or at room temperature.

Garnish with scallion greens.

Eileen Kammerer

MOM'S VEGETABLE BEEF BARLEY SOUP

We make this frequently all winter - always on Christmas Eve.
Serve with warm Kaiser rolls and butter. We often have a romaine, mandarin orange and almond salad and sometimes some cheeses on the side.

Yield: 6 - 8 servings

Ingredients
1 large can whole tomatoes
2 quarts water
2 beef shins with bones or soup bones and some lean beef cut in small pieces*
2 or 3 Idaho potatoes
1/4 c. barley
1 large bag frozen mixed vegetables
salt, pepper, chopped fresh parsley, and a little butter
*if you use shins, cut meat off bone in small pieces

Directions
In a large pot, melt butter then add meat pieces and soup bones. Brown all sides. Add 2 quarts water and the juice from the canned tomatoes. Simmer 1 hour. Add 1/4 cup barley. Simmer another hour. Add tomatoes (crush them first). Simmer for 45 minutes. Add potatoes, peeled and cut into 1 inch chunks. Add frozen vegetables. Bring to boil then immediately turn down and simmer for 15 minutes or until potatoes are tender. Salt and pepper to taste. Add chopped parsley toward the end of cooking time.

Elizabeth Edwards

PUMPKIN,CORN AND LIME SOUP

We served this soup at the St. George's 2003 Progressive Dinner. It is delicious, easy to make and very healthy: only 115 calories and 3 grams of fat per serving.

Yield: 6 servings

Ingredients
2 tsp. olive oil
1 large onion, chopped
1 medium red bell pepper, chopped
2 cloves garlic, chopped
2 tsp. ground cumin
1/2 tsp. cinnamon
1/4 tsp. salt
1/4 tsp. freshly ground pepper

1/8 tsp. ground red pepper
1 can (15 oz.) plain pumpkin
3 1/2 c. vegetable broth
1 c. frozen corn kernels
1/2 tsp. lime peel
1 tbsp. lime juice

Directions

Heat the oil in a Dutch oven over medium heat. Cook the onion, bell pepper and garlic until tender (about 12 minutes), stirring frequently. Add the cumin, cinnamon, salt, black pepper and ground red pepper. Cook and stir for about 30 seconds. Stir in the pumpkin and broth. Increase the heat to high and bring to a simmer. Reduce the heat to low, cover and simmer, stirring occasionally, for about 15 minutes. Stir in the corn, cover and cook for 5 more minutes. Remove from heat, stir in the lime peel and lime juice.

Terry Mc Farland

PUMPKIN SOUP

Delicious with leftovers at Thanksgiving or Christmas.

Yield: 6 - 8 servings

Ingredients

1- 1 lb. can of pumpkin or precook and mash one small pumpkin to make 2 cups
2 tbsp. butter
1/4 c. green peppers, chopped
2 tbsp. each of onion, parsley and thyme
1- 8 oz. can of tomatoes, chopped
2 c. chicken broth
1 tbsp. flour
1 c. of milk or half-and-half
1 bay leaf
salt and pepper to taste

Directions

Melt butter in a large saucepan. Add green peppers, onions, parsley, thyme and bay leaf. Brown for 5 minutes. Add can of tomatoes, pumpkin and chicken broth. Cover and simmer 30 minutes, stirring occasionally. Blend together 1 tbsp. flour and 1 c. milk or half-and-half and salt and pepper. Add to other ingredients, cook stirring until it comes to a boil. Remove bay leaf and then blend in a blender until smooth. Cool and refrigerate or freeze.

To double the recipe for 12 people: use 1 large can of pumpkin or 2 (1 lb. ones). Double all other ingredients except thyme.

Kate Gibbons

SENEGALESE CHICKEN SOUP

Yield: Serves 6 - 8

Ingredients
1 large onion diced
4 tbsp. olive oil
1 tsp. chopped garlic
6 tbsp. curry powder
1-2 tsp. cayenne pepper
2 tsp. ground coriander
5 c. chicken broth (Campbell's)
2- 28 oz. cans of Redpack crushed tomatoes in puree
1/2 c. smooth peanut butter
1 lb. cooked white chicken meat
1 c. scallions, sliced thinly
chopped peanuts for garnish

Directions
Cook onions in oil until soft and translucent. Add garlic and cook two minutes. Add curry powder, cayenne pepper and coriander and fry for an additional two minutes. (If dry, add a small amount of oil until moist). Add chicken broth and scrape bottom very well with a wooden spoon. Add tomatoes, salt and pepper. Simmer for 30 minutes. Stir often, scraping bottom every few minutes. Do not boil.

After the simmer period, measure two cups of the soup and in small increments stir the broth into the peanut butter until the peanut butter is smoothly incorporated. (If you want, you can use a blender instead). When smooth, add this puree to remaining soup and stir well. Add cooked chicken and scallions and cook for 5 minutes longer. Serve garnished with the chopped peanuts.

(Variations: I have also sautéed raw chicken breast with the onions and left to cook in the broth. Also, leftover rice added works well to make this a main course soup.)

Bryn Thompson

SHE CRAB SOUP

A favorite recipe from my grandmother!

Yield: 4 dinner-size servings

Ingredients
1 can green pea soup
1 can beef consommé soup

1 can tomato soup
1 pt. half and half
1 tsp. curry powder
1/4 c. sherry wine
1 lb. can (or more) crab meat

Directions

Heat together green pea soup, beef consommé and tomato soup. Do not let boil and do not dilute. Then add the rest of the ingredients. You may heat the crab separately in a little milk so as not to chill the soup, and then add it to the soup.

Jennifer Robelo

STRACCIATELLE SOUP

Stracciatelle means "torn rags", which is what the eggs look like when you stir them into the hot broth. This soup is my favorite version of Italian Wedding Soup.

Yield: Serves 6 - 8. Recipe can be doubled.

Ingredients

Soup:
1 quart College Inn chicken broth
2 c. water
1/2 c. pastina
1 tsp. fresh parsley, chopped
1 carrot, thinly sliced
1/2 lb. spinach or escarole (leafy part, julienne cut)

Meatballs:
1/2 lb. ground beef
1 egg
2 tsp. grated cheese
2 tsp. fresh parsley, chopped
1 small onion, chopped

Finishing:
2 eggs
grated cheese

Directions

In a soup pot, combine soup ingredients and bring to a low boil. Mix meatball ingredients in a bowl, make tiny meatballs and drop into boiling broth mixture. In a small bowl, beat 2 eggs. With a wooden spoon, stir soup as you slowly drop in the eggs, stirring constantly. Remove from heat. Cover and let stand for 2 minutes.

Donna DiPaulo

STRAWBERRY SOUP

Yield: 6 - 8 servings

Ingredients

8 tsp. cornstarch
4 c. milk
1/2 c. sugar
12 oz. strawberries, pureed

Directions

Dissolve cornstarch in 1 cup milk in large 2 quart saucepan. Stir in remaining milk and sugar. Cook over medium heat, stirring constantly until mixture starts to thicken - 15 to 18 minutes.

Add strawberry puree and stir until consistency of thin pancake batter - about 5 minutes. Serve warm or chilled.

Mildred H. Burns

THE BEST BARBECUE SAUCE

Great with pulled pork or sliced thin roast beef and served on a roll.

Ingredients

2 bottles chili sauce
1 can tomato sauce
2 tbsp. vinegar
2 tbsp. brown sugar
1/3 c. lemon juice
1 tsp. dry mustard
1 tsp. tabasco or other hot sauce
1/2 c. olive oil
2 c. chopped onion
1/3 c. water
2 bay leaves
pulled pork or thinly sliced beef

Directions

Combine all ingredients. Bring to a boil and then simmer for 30 minutes.

Add pulled pork or thinly sliced beef. Serve on a crusty roll.

Nancy Murphy

TORTELLINI SOUP

This recipe reheats very nicely.

Yield: 8 servings

Ingredients
1 lb. frozen rainbow tortellini with cheese
6 cans non fat-low sodium chicken broth (14 1/2 oz.)
4 cloves garlic, minced
3 bunches scallions, cut in rounds
1 can crushed tomatoes
salt and pepper to taste
2 c. chopped spinach
1 tsp. dried basil
1 tsp. olive oil

Directions
Sauté garlic till tender. Add chicken broth, scallions, basil, salt and pepper to taste. Bring to a boil and then reduce the heat and simmer for 5 minutes. Add spinach and tomatoes, simmer for 5 minutes. Add cheese tortellini and simmer till cooked. The tortellini comes to the top when it is done.

Serve with Italian bread.

Richard Coyle

VEGETABLE BEEF SOUP WITH BARLEY, FOR A CROWD

A hearty meal in itself.

Ingredients
3 lb. chicken steaks or round steak
3 large cans of beef broth (48 oz.)
3 lb. frozen soup veggies
2 cans diced tomatoes (14 oz.)
1 c. barley
3 tbsp. minced garlic
olive oil
A-1 sauce
garlic powder

Directions

Cut steaks into medium size pieces. Start cooking in olive oil (1-2 tbsp.). Sprinkle with garlic powder and cook with A-1 sauce (enough to make a gravy). When steak is about medium rare add beef broth, minced garlic, frozen vegetables, and diced tomatoes. Cover and cook over low for about 2 hours. Adjust seasoning to taste. I add Minor's beef extract for a beefier flavor. Add barley in the last 1/2 hour of cooking.

This soup gets more flavorful with cooking. It freezes well in quart containers for giving away or future use.

Richard Coyle

WHITE BEAN, HAM AND TOMATO SOUP

Quick. Can be frozen in smaller amounts.

Yield: 6 - 8 servings

Ingredients

2 c. diced sweet onions
2 tbsp. olive oil
1- 48 oz. can of chicken broth
1- 28 oz. can of plum tomatoes, drained and diced
2- 16 oz. cans of white beans, drained and rinsed
1 c. diced boiled or baked ham

Directions

Cook and stir onions in oil for 4 - 5 minutes or until soft. Add all other ingredients, bring to a boil. Lower the heat and simmer for 30 minutes.

Cool a little, then refrigerate or freeze when cold.

Kate Gibbons

Salads &
Vegetables

BAKED ACORN SQUASH (STUFFED)

A winter vegetable dish from the previous St. George's Cookbook.

Yield: 6 servings

Ingredients
3 medium acorn squash
1/2 tsp. salt
1/4 tsp. nutmeg
1 c. soft bread crumbs
1/8 tsp. pepper
1 lb. sausage meat
1/2 c. diced onion
1/4 in. boiling water in baking pan

Directions
Wash squash, cut in half lengthwise and remove seeds and fibers. Place in baking dish, cut side down. Pour 1/4 inch of water into bottom of baking dish. Bake at 425 degrees for 30 minutes. Turn squash over and sprinkle with mixture of salt, pepper and nutmeg. Mix remaining ingredients together and spoon into squash.

Place into pan with 1/4 inch of boiling water. Reduce to 350 degrees and bake for 35 minutes or until squash is tender.

Helen Lungren

BARBARA'S ORANGE CHICKEN SALAD

This recipe was given to me by a former teaching associate.

Yield: 4 servings

Ingredients
4 c. chicken, cooked and cut into pieces
2 c. thinly sliced celery
1 c. walnuts
1 c. fresh orange sections
1 can of orange juice concentrate
1/4 c. mayonnaise
1 orange
1/4 tsp. Tabasco sauce
salt to taste
1 c. heavy cream

Directions

Mix together and refrigerate:
4 c. chicken, cooked and cut into pieces
2 c. thinly sliced celery
1 c. walnuts
1 c. fresh orange sections

Mix dressing:
1/4 c. thawed orange juice concentrate
1/4 c. mayonnaise
grated rind of 1 orange
1/4 tsp. Tabasco sauce
salt to taste
1 c. of heavy cream, whipped

Toss the salad with the dressing just before serving

Karen Schloesser

BOB TREMPE'S CREAMY CAESAR DRESSING (LOW CHOLESTEROL)

A recipe from a very good golfing buddy.

Yield: 8 servings

Ingredients
8 garlic cloves (crushed)
1 1/2 c. salad oil (I use half light olive oil & half regular salad oil)
juice of 3 - 4 fresh lemons
1 small (2 eggs) container of egg substitute (Egg Beaters)
1 can flat anchovies, drained
1 tbsp. Dijon mustard
1 tbsp. Worcestershire sauce
1/3 c. grated cheese (Parmesan or Romano)
salt & pepper to taste

Directions
Combine all ingredients in a bowl and blend until entirely smooth. I use a Braun hand blender. I've never tried using a regular blender. I assume it would work.

We like to make the salad "dry" putting it on individual salad plates. Top with croutons and sliced extra anchovies to taste. Then spoon a couple of tablespoons of dressing on top and sprinkle with extra cheese.

Claire Coyle

BROCCOLI CASSEROLE

This dish can be made ahead of time and refrigerated but it may take a little longer to cook.

Yield: 6 servings

Ingredients
2 pkgs. frozen chopped broccoli
1 can mushroom soup
1 c. grated sharp cheddar cheese
2 tbsp. chopped onion
3/4 c. mayonnaise
2 slightly beaten eggs
10 Ritz crackers
butter

Directions
Cook the broccoli in salted water. Mix soup, mayonnaise, eggs, cheese and onion. Fold broccoli into mixture after draining and put into a buttered 1 1/2 qt. casserole dish. Dot with butter and sprinkle with crushed Ritz crackers.

Bake uncovered in a 350 degree oven for 45 minutes.

Jennifer Robelo

BROCCOLI SALAD

A popular pot luck salad

Yield: 10 - 12 servings

Ingredients
4 bunches broccoli
1 lb. bacon, fried and crumbled
1/2 c. raisins
1/2 c. onions, chopped fine
2 c. mayonnaise
1/2 c. sugar (fine)
3 tbsp. white vinegar

Directions
Mix mayonnaise, sugar, and vinegar. Add remaining ingredients, stir and refrigerate several hours before serving.

Stephanie Mahoney

BROILED VEGETABLE TERRINE

A Chris Smythe specialty which makes a beautiful and colorful presentation.

Yield: 6 servings

Ingredients
2 large red bell peppers, cored, seeded and cut into quarters
2 large yellow bell peppers, cored, seeded and cut into quarters
1 large eggplant, sliced lengthwise
2 large zucchini, sliced lengthwise
6 tbsp. olive oil
1 large red onion, thinly sliced
1/2 c. raisins
1 tbsp. tomato paste
1 tbsp. red wine vinegar
1 2/3 c. tomato juice
2 tbsp. powdered gelatin
fresh basil leaves, to garnish

Dressing
6 tbsp. extra virgin olive oil
2 tbsp. red wine vinegar
salt and ground pepper

Directions
Place the prepared red and yellow peppers skin side up under a hot broiler and cook until the skins are blackened. Then transfer them to a bowl, cover them and let them cool. Arrange the eggplant and the zucchini slices on separate baking sheets. Brush them with a little oil and cook them under the broiler, turning occasionally, until tender and golden. Heat the remaining olive oil in a frying pan and add the sliced onion, raisins, tomato paste and red wine vinegar. Cook gently until soft and syrupy. Then let the mixture cool in the frying pan. Line a 7 1/2 cup terrine with plastic wrap (oil the terrine lightly first) leaving a little hanging over on the sides.

Pour half the tomato juice into a saucepan and sprinkle with the gelatin. Dissolve gently over low heat, stirring. Place a layer of red peppers in the bottom of the terrine and pour in enough tomato juice with gelatin to cover. Continue layering the eggplant, zucchini, yellow peppers and onion mixture, finishing with another layer of red peppers. Pour tomato juice over each layer of vegetables. Add the remaining tomato juice to any left in the pan and pour into the terrine. Give it a sharp tap to disperse the juice. Cover the terrine and chill until set.

To make the dressing, whisk together the oil and vinegar and season to taste with salt and pepper. Turn out the terrine and remove the plastic wrap. Serve in thick slices, drizzled with dressing. Garnish with basil leaves.

Bryn Smythe

BUFFALO JUNE'S POTATO SALAD

A blast from the past St. George's cookbook.

Yield: 6 servings

Ingredients
6 - 8 white baking potatoes
1 c. mayonnaise (more or less-adjust to taste)
1/2 medium green pepper
1/4 to 1/2 small white Spanish sweet onion
1 - 2 stalks celery
Jane's Krazy Mixed Up Salt or regular salt to taste
pepper to taste

Directions
Wash and brush potatoes. Boil baking potatoes with skins on until firm when fork tested. Cool on platter, peel and cut into cubes. Finely chop green pepper, onion and celery. Add to cooled potatoes. Add salt and pepper to mayonnaise and mix into vegetables.

Garnish with hard boiled eggs, fresh parsley and paprika.

June McKendrick

CAJUN BEANS & RICE

My mother is from Louisiana!

Yield: 6 - 8 servings

Ingredients
1 tbsp. butter or margarine
1 tbsp. flour
1- 15 1/2 oz. can stewed tomatoes
1- 19 oz. can red kidney beans
1 small onion and/or green pepper, diced - optional
black pepper or cayenne pepper

Directions
At medium heat, melt butter in frying pan. Cook onion and/or pepper until soft. Add flour and stir constantly (approximately 2 minutes) to make a "roux" (thickener). Pour in can of tomatoes and can of beans (rinse the beans first!). Heat through, until beans are completely warm and cooked. Season with pepper, as desired. Serve over rice.

Schaunel Steinnagel

CHICKEN SALAD DI PIETRO

Yield: 6 servings

Ingredients
2 lbs. boneless chicken breasts
1 lb. frozen white corn niblets
1 c. ranch dressing
1 small yellow onion, Vedallia if possible
6 large ripe tomatoes

Directions
Grill 2 lbs. boneless chicken breasts. Let cool and dice.

In a mixing bowl, add chicken, 1 cup of ranch dressing, one small yellow minced onion, 1 lb. of frozen corn "niblets" and 1 tsp. fresh minced garlic. Season to taste. Mix well.

Scoop out 6 large ripe tomatoes and discard seeds, etc. Stuff the tomatoes with the chicken mixture and let cool overnight. Each stuffed tomato is one serving.

Pete Ricci

CRUNCHY MANDARIN SALAD

We first tried this recipe at a St. George's Lenten Supper and everyone really enjoyed it. It doesn't keep well, so plan to eat all you make.

Yield: 10 servings

Ingredients
1 tsp. salt
1/2 tsp. pepper
4 tbsp. sugar
1/2 c. salad oil
4 tbsp. vinegar
couple of dashes Tabasco
2 tbsp. snipped parsley
1/2 c. sliced slivered almonds
4 tbsp. sugar
1 head of lettuce
1 head of romaine
1 1/2 c. celery, chopped
4 green onions, thinly sliced
2- 11 oz. cans of mandarin oranges, drained

Directions

Shake first 7 ingredients in a covered jar; refrigerate. Cook almonds and sugar over medium low heat, stirring until sugar is melted and almonds are coated. Cool on wax paper, break apart and store at room temperature.

Wash lettuce and romaine and tear it. Place greens in a plastic bag, add celery and onions; refrigerate.

5 minutes before serving, add dressing and orange slices to bag. Shake until well coated. Add almonds and shake.

Coeli Wagner

CURRIED COUSCOUS

This is a delicious side dish with chicken, lamb, pork, and salmon. It's tasty and you can add your own favorite ingredients to make it special in different ways.

Yield: 6 - 8 servings

Ingredients
1 1/2 c. couscous
1 tbsp. unsalted butter
1 1/2 c. boiling water
1/4 c. plain yogurt
1/4 c. good olive oil
1 tsp. white wine vinegar
1 tsp. curry powder
1/4 tsp. ground turmeric
1 1/2 tsp. kosher salt
1 tsp freshly ground black pepper
1/2 c. small-diced carrots
1/2 c. minced fresh flat-leaf parsley
1/2 c. dried currents
1/2 c. raisins
1/2 c. blanched, sliced almonds
2 scallions, thinly sliced
1/4 c. small-diced red onion

Add any or all of the following ~ dried cherries, dried dates, dried cranberries, dried figs, chopped fresh mint, etc.

Directions

Place couscous in medium bowl. Melt butter in boiling water and pour over couscous. Cover with Saran Wrap and allow couscous to soak for 5 minutes. Fluff with fork.

Whisk together yogurt, olive oil, vinegar, curry, turmeric, salt, and pepper.

Pour over fluffed couscous, and mix well with fork.

Add carrots, parsley, currants, almonds, scallions, and red onions, and mix well. Season to taste.

Serve at room temperature.

Randy Klein

GREAT SUMMER SALAD

Yield: 6 - 8 servings

Ingredients
1 c. oil
1/2 c. sugar
1/3 c. white vinegar
1 tbsp. dry mustard
1 tbsp. celery seed
1 tsp. salt
1 avocado
1 pint strawberries
2 green onions, sliced
1 head Boston lettuce
1 bag baby spinach

Directions

Blend first six ingredients in blender and chill for at least one hour. Chop avocado, strawberries, and green onions. Mix Boston lettuce and spinach in bowl and add avocado mixture. Add dressing (amount to taste) immediately prior to serving. Enjoy!

The Vantre Family

Helpful Hints

Fresh tomatoes keep longer if stored with the stems down.

GRILLED ZUCCHINI IN BALSAMIC MARINADE

Yield: 6 - 8 servings

Ingredients
8 zucchini (2 lbs) cut diagonally in 1/2 inch strips
1/3 cup plus 2 tbsp. extra virgin olive oil
2 tbsp. balsamic vinegar
1 tbsp. red wine vinegar
1 garlic clove, crushed in press
1/4 tsp. salt
1/4 tsp. ground black pepper
1 tbsp. chopped fresh mint leaves

Directions
Prepare charcoal grill - when coals turn white, spread them evenly. In a large bowl, toss zucchini with 2 tbsp. olive oil. Grill zucchini, turning once until just tender (approximately 5 minutes).

Transfer to serving platter. In medium bowl whisk together balsamic vinegar, red wine vinegar, garlic, salt and pepper. Gradually whisk in remaining 1/3 cup olive oil. Pour over the zucchini and let stand until the zucchini is cool.

Cover tightly with plastic wrap and marinate at room temperature for at least 4 hours.

Serve at room temperature (can be prepared up to 3 days ahead and refrigerated - remove from refrigerator 1 hour before serving).

Elizabeth Edwards

MANDARIN SALAD

This recipe was given to me by my Aunt Marie Thompson at my bridal shower. It is a great summer recipe and it can be used as a meal by adding grilled chicken!

Yield: 4 - 6 servings

Ingredients
Sweet & Sour Dressing:
1/4 c. vegetable oil
2 tbsp. sugar
2 tbsp. red wine vinegar

1 tbsp. snipped parsley
1/2 tsp. salt
dash pepper
dash hot pepper sauce

Salad:
1/2 head of Romaine lettuce torn into bite-sized pieces
1/2 c. sliced almonds
2 green scallions, sliced thin
1 can (11 oz.) mandarin orange sections, drained

Directions

Put all dressing ingredients into a tightly covered jar and shake well to mix. Keep refrigerated.

Toss Romaine with dressing just before serving. Add almonds, scallions, and mandarin oranges.

April D. Chester

MELCHOR'S SCALLOPED POTATOES

A scrumptious and easy recipe from my brother-in-law.

Yield: 8 - 10 servings

Ingredients
3 lbs. potatoes (preferably Yukon Gold)
1 pt. Half 'n Half
1 c. shredded Swiss or cheddar cheese
salt, coarse pepper, parsley flakes

Directions

Scrub potatoes and then slice into thin rounds, leaving connected at bottom. Place potatoes in 13 x 9 inch pan with uncut edge down. Season with salt, pepper, and parsley flakes.

Pour Half 'n Half over potatoes, cover with foil and bake until potatoes are tender (about 1 hour at 375 degrees).

Uncover and sprinkle cheese on top - return to oven and bake uncovered until cheese is melted and brown and bubbly.

Eileen Kammerer

MOM'S VINAIGRETTE COLE SLAW

The only cole slaw I ever make!

Yield: 6 - 8 servings

Ingredients
1 head of cabbage
1 small onion (optional)
pimento-stuffed green olives
parsley (finely chopped)
3 tbsp. vegetable oil
1 tbsp. white vinegar (can use different binder, i.e., rice vinegar or tarragon vinegar, etc.)
1 tsp. sugar
1/2 tsp. salt

Directions
Cut the cabbage in quarters. Slice cabbage as finely as you can with a sharp knife. Do the same with onion. Slice olives across in thin slices. Combine all with parsley.

Combine oil, vinegar, salt, and sugar in jar and mix. Toss dressing with slaw shortly before serving.

Elizabeth Edwards

PATTI'S GREEN BEANS

A great dish for a buffet dinner.

Yield: 8 - 10 people

Ingredients
1 medium white onion, chopped
1- 14 1/2 oz. can chopped tomatoes
1- 6 oz. can tomato paste
3/4 cup water
1 tbsp. olive oil
1 tbsp. chopped fresh oregano (or 1 1/2 tsp. dried)
1 clove garlic - chopped
1 lb. string beans - 2 inch length
seasoned salt
freshly ground black pepper
crushed red pepper flakes
1 c. shredded Taco four-cheese blend

Directions

In a Dutch oven, combine onion, tomatoes with juice, tomato paste, water, olive oil, oregano and garlic. Stir well to dissolve tomato paste.

Add the string beans and season with salt, black pepper and red pepper flakes. Bring to boil over medium heat. Cover and cook until beans are very tender and are swimming in a thick tomato sauce. I prefer the beans firmer but both ways are good.

Remove from heat and add cheese blend. Mix thoroughly with beans and sauce.

Cover and allow cheeses to melt. Serve and enjoy.

Richard Coyle

QUICK DILL PICKLES

Always a hit for nibbling or on a sandwich or hamburger.

Yield: approximately 2 quarts.

Ingredients

4-6 Kirby cucumbers or whatever kind available
1 small bunch of fresh dill
12 whole black peppercorns
1 c. white vinegar
1 tsp. salt
1/4 c. sugar
1 clove garlic, sliced

Directions

Cut the cucumbers into 1 in. square chunks or 1/8 in. slices after scoring with a fork. Place in a heat proof bowl with 12 - 15 springs of dill. Place peppercorns, vinegar, salt and sugar in small sauce pan over medium heat.

Cook until salt and sugar dissolve (approximately 1 - 2 minutes). Add garlic and bring to a boil.

Remove from heat and pour hot mixture over the cucumbers. Let stand to 30 - 40 minutes. Cool in the fridge before serving.

Dolores Jaquith

QUICK-N-EASY MUSTARD VINAIGRETTE

This dressing will dress up any salad.

Yield: 1 cup

Ingredients
4 tbsp. red wine vinegar
1 tbsp. Dijon mustard
1 tsp. sugar
1/2 tsp. salt
1/2 tsp. pepper
1/2 c. olive oil
herbs to taste

Directions
Whisk together vinegar, mustard, sugar, salt and pepper. Drizzle in oil while continuing to whisk. Add herbs to taste. Whisk again just prior to serving.

Store leftovers in the refrigerator. Bring to room temperature before using.

Kristen Kucharczuk

RATATOUILLE

A summer favorite from the old St. George's Cookbook.

Yield: 4 servings

Ingredients
1 medium onion, sliced
1/2 medium green pepper, sliced
1/6 c. oil
1 clove garlic, finely chopped
1 small eggplant, peeled and cubed
2 medium tomatoes, chopped
1 medium zucchini, thinly sliced
1/2 c. V-8 juice
1 tsp. basil
1 tsp. parsley flakes
1/2 tsp. salt
1/8 tsp. pepper

Directions

In a 2 1/2 quart casserole combine onion, green pepper, oil and garlic. Microwave on high 4 - 5 minutes, stirring once. Add remaining ingredients and heat covered, 18 - 20 minutes on high until vegetables are tender, stirring occasionally. Let stand covered 5 minutes before serving.

Mary Beumer

ROASTED RED POTATOES

Roasted potatoes are an ideal side. The preparation is very, very easy - simply toss the ingredients and cook in the oven.

Yield: Serves 4
Preparation Time: 15 minutes
Cooking Time: 40 minutes

Ingredients

6 red potatoes, large, cut into small chunks with skins on
2 tsp. olive oil
1/2 tsp. pepper, black, fresh ground
1 tsp. salt, kosher
generous sprinkle of garlic powder

Directions

Begin by preheating the oven to 425 degrees. Place the just-cut potatoes in a bowl and toss them with the other ingredients. Once coated, spread them out over a parchment paper covered cookie sheet. Put in oven and cook for 40 minutes, or until tender and they begin to brown.

Richard Coyle

Helpful Hints

When cooking corn on the cob, add a little milk and a dash of sugar to the cooking water

---

SALAD WITH HONEY MUSTARD DRESSING

Yield: 10 - 12 servings

Ingredients
1 c. vegetable oil
1/2 c. plus 3 tbsp. sugar, divided
1/4 c. vinegar
1/4 c. honey
2 tbsp. lemon juice
1 tbsp. onion powder
1 tsp. salt
1 tsp. celery seed
1 tsp. ground mustard
1 tsp. paprika
1/2 c. slivered almonds
9 c. torn Romaine
1 c. shredded cheddar cheese
2 hard cooked eggs, diced

Directions
In saucepan combine oil, 1/2 cup sugar, vinegar, honey, lemon juice, and seasonings. Cook and stir until sugar dissolves - cool.

In skillet over low heat cook almonds and remaining sugar until nuts are glazed - cool.

In salad bowl, toss Romaine (or other greens) with cheese and almonds. Top with eggs. Drizzle with dressing and serve.

Dolores Jacquith

SALMON SALAD

There are many recipes for salmon salad. This delicious favorite is easy to prepare

Yield: 4 - 6 servings

Ingredients
2 lbs. cooked salmon, chilled
1 c. small-diced celery (3 stalks)
1/2 c. small-diced onion (1 small onion)
2 tbsp. minced fresh dill
2 tbsp. capers, drained

2 tbsp. raspberry vinegar
2 tbsp. good olive oil
1/2 tsp. kosher salt
1/2 tsp.freshly ground black pepper

Directions

Break salmon into large flakes. Remove skin and bones and place salmon in bowl. Add celery, red onion, dill, capers, raspberry vinegar, olive oil, salt, and paper.

Season to taste. Mix well and serve cold or at room temperature.

Randy Klein

SEA BREEZE SALAD

A refreshing and tasty gelatin salad, popular at Easter time and at potluck suppers. I found this recipe in 1967 (the year we were married) and we've been enjoying it ever since.

Yield: 10 - 12 servings

Ingredients

2- 3 oz packages lime flavored gelatin
1 1/2 c. hot water
1 c. evaporated milk
1- 3 oz. package cream cheese, cubed
4 ice cubes
2 tbsp. lemon juice
1- 8 3/4 oz. can crushed pineapple
1/2 c. pecans or walnuts
1/8 tsp. salt

Directions

In a blender "grind" gelatin and water for 40 seconds. Add milk, cream cheese, ice cubes, and lemon juice and "grind" 20 seconds. Add pineapple, pecans, and salt and "grind" 5 seconds.

Turn into a 2 quart mold and chill until firm.

Betty Duffey

Helpful Hints

A simple dressing for fruit salad is grated orange rind and orange juice stirred into sour cream.

SHRIMP SALAD

I serve this with cheese biscuits and fresh fruit for dessert. Nice summer luncheon.

Yield: 6 servings

Ingredients
3 c. shell macaroni, cooked
1 large onion, chopped
1/2 c. celery, chopped
1 small jar stuffed olives
25 - 30 medium cooked shrimp (cleaned & de-veined)
1/2 c. or more mayonnaise
salt & pepper to taste
lettuce
cherry tomatoes
deviled eggs
paprika

Directions
Mix all ingredients together. Serve on a bed of lettuce. Surround with cherry tomatoes and deviled eggs. Sprinkle with paprika.

Helen Lungren

SPAGHETTI - BEAN SPROUT SALAD

Do-ahead and chill for 3 hours.

Yield: 8 - 10 servings

Ingredients
Sauce:
3/4 c. mayonnaise
1 tbsp. soy sauce
1 tsp. salt
1 tsp. garlic powder
dash of black pepper

Salad:
7 oz. vermicelli, cooked and drained
1- 16 oz. can bean sprouts, drained
1- 4oz. can mushrooms, drained
1/2 c. celery, chopped

1/3 c. green pepper, chopped
1/4 c. onion, chopped (optional)
1 c. frozen uncooked peas
1/2 . cashews

Directions

Mix sauce ingredients together. Mix all other ingredients together except the nuts. Add this mixture to the sauce. Refrigerate for at least 3 hours. Add the cashews before servings.

Karen Schloesser

SPICY SESAME NOODLES

Big hit at cookouts.

Yield: 6 servings or as a side dish will serve about 10
Definitely make a day ahead.

Ingredients

Noodle Ingredients:
2 tbsp. salt
1 lb. thin linguine or other thin pasta
1/4 c. peanut oil
1 c. Sesame Mayonnaise (see below)
Szechuan hot chili oil
8 scallions (green onions), trimmed, cleaned and cut diagonally into 1/2 inch pieces
blanched asparagus tips, broccoli, snow peas or cashew nuts (for garnish) - I use the nuts

Sesame Mayonnaise ingredients:
1 whole egg
2 egg yolks
2 1/2 tbsp. rice vinegar
2 1/2 tbsp. oriental soy sauce
3 tbsp prepared Dijon style mustard
1/4 c. dark oriental sesame oil
 2 1/2 c. corn oil
Szechuan-style hot and spicy oil or Mongolian Fire Oil (optional - I use)
grated fresh orange rind (optional - I don't use)

Directions

Noodle directions:
1. Bring 4 quarts of water to a full boil in a large pot, stir in salt, drop in the linguine,

and cook until tender but not mushy. Drain, toss in a mixing bowl with the peanut oil, and let cool to room temperature.

2. Whisk together the Sesame Mayonnaise and chili oil to taste in a small bowl. Do not hesitate to make the mayonnaise quite spicy, the noodles will absorb a lot of heat.

3. Add the scallions to the pasta, pour in the sesame mayonnaise, and toss gently but well. Cover and refrigerate until serving time.

4. Toss the noodles again and add additional sesame mayonnaise if they seem dry. Arrange in a shallow serving bowl and garnish with asparagus, broccoli, snow peas or cashews, if desired.

Sesame Mayonnaise directions:
1. In a food processor fitted with a steel blade (I use a blender) process the whole egg, egg yolks, vinegar, soy sauce and mustard for 1 minute.

2. With the motor running, dribble in sesame oil and then corn oil in a slow, steady stream.

3. Season with drops of the hot and spicy oil if you use it, and scrape the mayonnaise out into a bowl. Cover and refrigerate until ready to use.

Yield: about 3 1/2 cups mayonnaise - enough for 2 lbs. of pasta

Claire Coyle

SPINACH CASSEROLE

Can be made ahead except for stuffing - add just before baking.

Yield: 10 servings.

Ingredients
2 packages frozen chopped spinach
1 c. chopped onions
2 cans cream of mushroom soup
2 eggs beaten
2 c. shredded cheddar cheese
2 c. Pepperidge Farm stuffing

Directions
Cook spinach according to package directions, drain, and cool. Add other ingredients. Bake 1 hour at 350 degrees in covered 3 quart casserole.

Helen Dalstrom

SPINACH SALAD

An old St. George's Cookbook favorite that you will love.

Yield: 8 - 10 servings

Ingredients
1 head lettuce
1 lb. fresh spinach
1 can (6 oz.) cashews

Dressing:
1/3 c. sugar
1 tsp. salt
1 tsp. dry mustard
1 tsp. grated onion
1/4 c. vinegar
1 c. oil
1 tsp. celery seed

Directions
Dressing:
Mix sugar, salt, mustard and add onion and vinegar and blend. Pour oil slowly into mixture and beat with an electric mixer slowly at the same time. Add celery seeds.

Wash, clean and tear lettuce and spinach. Place in a large salad bowl. Add the cashews and toss with the dressing.

Ruth Howes

TOMATO ASPIC

Easy and delicious too.

Yield: 8 - 10 servings

Ingredients
3 1/2 c. tomato juice
1/2 c. horseradish
2- 3 oz. packages lemon jello
2 tbsp. vinegar

Directions
Dissolve jello in boiling tomato juice. Add other ingredients - pour into mold. Chill until set.

Helen Dalstrom

TURKEY STUFFING

More interesting than the stovetop mixes.

Yield: 6 - 8 servings

Ingredients
1 package of cubed bread
2 - 3 cans chicken broth
2 apples, coarsely chopped
1 c. raisins
3/4 c. pecans chopped

Directions
Mix all ingredients and place in lightly oiled casserole. Bake at 375 degrees for 40 minutes.

Mary Lou Toal

UNCLE BOB'S ANTLER POTATOES

In his time, my Uncle Bob was a great cook. This is one of his favorites and ours also. Not for cholesterol watchers. Goes best with red meats cooked medium rare. It will definitely hold its own with a good cabernet.

Yield: 6 - 8 servings

Ingredients
3 - 4 lbs potatoes (new or red skin)
1 tsp. salt
1/4 lb. butter
1 tbsp. dry mustard
freshly ground black pepper
1 can evaporated milk

Directions
Boil potatoes with skin on until firmly done. Remove skin while hot and dice. Keep in warm place.

In heavy skillet melt butter with salt and mustard over medium heat. Keep tilting pan back and forth as butter melts to mix salt and mustard. Continue tilting until butter starts to brown. Do not burn.

Remove from the heat and add potatoes. Using a wooden spoon, gently stir potatoes until all the butter is absorbed.

Sprinkle pepper generously, covering potatoes well. Put pan back on heat (medium) and start slowly adding milk over potatoes, constantly stirring.

Continue stirring until it starts to bubble and thicken to desired consistency, like a cream sauce. Adjust seasoning and serve.

Richard Coyle

VEGETABLE CASSEROLE

A tasty zucchini recipe

Yield: 6 - 8 servings

Ingredients
3 zucchini, cut into 1/4 inch slices
7 fresh tomatoes, skinned and cut into slices
2 large yellow onions,diced
Maggio Mozzarella cheese,diced
garlic salt to taste
olive oil
parmesan cheese

Directions
In a long casserole (approx. 13 inch) place the following:

1. A layer of zucchini cut into 1/4 inch slices on the bottom.
2. A layer of skinned, sliced tomatoes.
3. A layer of onions, diced and sprinkled over the tomatoes.
4. Sprinkle garlic salt and olive oil over the onion layer.
5. A layer of mozzarella cheese diced (layer a generous amount)
6. Shake parmesan cheese over the mozzarella layer.
7. Repeat #1-6 so you have 2 layers in the casserole

Bake the casserole in a 350-375 degree oven for 1 hour.

Karen Schloesser

Helpful Hints

A little soy sauce and curry powder added to mayonnaise for turkey or chicken salad adds zest for those who like a spicy salad

---

YUMMY SWEET POTATOES

Yield: 6 - 8 servings

Ingredients
6 large sweet potatoes
1/2 c. butter, melted
1 eggs, beaten
1/4 c. heavy cream
1/2 tsp. cinnamon
1 tsp. vanilla
1 tsp. salt
1/2 c. raisins
1/2 c. chopped pecans

Directions
Preheat oven to 425 degrees. Pierce sweet potatoes and bake on ungreased sheet until soft (about one hour) - cool. When cool enough to handle, peel and mash potatoes. Stir in butter, eggs, cream, cinnamon, vanilla, salt and raisins. Place in 13 x 9 inch baking dish. Top with pecans. Bake at 350 degrees for 30 minutes.

Helen Lungren

Helpful Hints

To clean spinach quickly, wash it in fairly warm water.

Main Courses

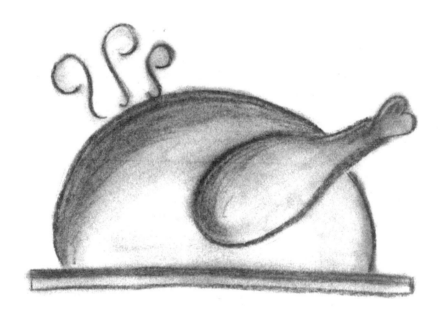

BAKED TILAPIA WITH TOMATOES AND OLIVES

Yield : 6 servings
Wine Suggestions: Riesling, Chardonnay or Rose (French)

Ingredients
6 tilapia fillets
1/4 c. extra-virgin olive oil
4 sprigs of fresh thyme
3 tomatoes peeled, seeded and chopped
1/2 c. coarsely chopped green olives
1/4 tsp. dried hot red pepper flakes
2 garlic cloves, minced
1/2 c. finely chopped red onion
1 tbsp. fresh lime juice

Directions
Preheat oven to 400 degrees. Lightly oil a shallow baking dish, large enough to hold fillets in one layer.

In a bowl stir together the oil, the thyme, the tomatoes, the olives, the red pepper flakes, the garlic, the onion, and the lime juice. In the prepared baking dish arrange the fillets, skin sides down, season them with salt and spoon the tomato mixture over them. Bake the fish, uncovered, in the middle of the oven 15 - 20 minutes, or until it just flakes.

Note: If the skin is removed, I place the fillets in a bed of the mixture and put the remainder on the top of the fillets.

Richard Coyle

BEEF AND BROCCOLI OR SPINACH

A quick dinner.

Yield: 4 servings
Wine Suggestions: Cabernet Sauvignon, Merlot, Syrah or Zinfandel.

Ingredients
3/4 lb. boneless beef sirloin steak
1 tbsp. olive oil
1 tsp. minced garlic
1 medium onion, cut into medium wedges

1 can of Campbell's Golden Mushroom soup
1/2 c. water
1 tbsp. soy sauce
2 c. broccoli flowerlets or 2 boxes leaf spinach

Directions

Slice the beef across the grain into very thin strips. In skillet over medium heat in hot oil, cook the beef and garlic until the beef is browned. Add the onion and cook for 5 minutes, stirring often. Stir in the soup, water and soy sauce. Heat to boiling. Add broccoli. Reduce heat to low. Cover and simmer for 5 minutes or until the vegetables are just tender.

Serve over noodles, rice, couscous or pearl barley.

Note: to substitute spinach for broccoli, add 2 boxes of leaf spinach, thawed and squeezed. Left over cooked vegetables may also be added and heated through just before serving.

Kate Gibbons

CAMPECHE BAKED FISH FILLETS WITH TOMATO, HABANERA AND CITRUS

A recipe presented at one of the "Men Cook" evenings held at St. George's.

Yield: 4 servings

Wine Suggestions: Riesling, Pinot Gris or Chardonnay.

Ingredients

1/4 c. fresh sour orange juice or 2 - 3 tbsp. lime juice
2 tbsp. chopped cilantro
4- 5 - 6 oz. fish fillets or steaks (we used orange roughy)

Sauce:
1 1/2 lbs. ripe tomatoes (3 medium large or 9 - 12 plum tomatoes)
1 1/2 tbsp. olive oil
1 small white onion, thinly sliced
1-2 fresh habanera chilies, stems removed and halved
salt (about 1/4 tsp.)

Directions

Sauce:
Roast tomatoes on a baking sheet 4 inches below a very hot broiler until blackened on

one side, about 6 minutes, then flip and roast on the other side. Cool and peel, collecting all juices with the tomatoes. Coarsely puree the tomatoes (with juices) in a food processor. In a deep, heavy skillet or medium size saucepan, heat the oil over medium heat. Add the onion and fry until beginning to brown, about 6 minutes. Increase the heat to medium-high and when hot, add tomatoes and chile. Stir for 5 minutes as the mixture sears and boils rapidly, then reduce the heat to medium low and simmer for about 15 minutes, until medium thick. Season with salt.

Baking the fish:
Turn on the oven to 350 degrees. Lay out the fish on a highly oiled baking dish. Do not overlap fish. Drizzle with sour orange juice or lime juice and sprinkle with cilantro. Spoon the warm tomato sauce over the fish and bake until the fish just flakes when pressed firmly, about 10 - 15 minutes.

With a spatula, remove the fillets to a warm serving platter. Thoroughly mix the sauce and juices that remain in the baking dish, then spoon them over the fish. Garnish with sprigs of cilantro and serve at once.

Chris Smythe

CARIBBEAN CHICKEN SALAD

A favorite wherever we go!

Yield: 6 - 8 servings
Wine Suggestions: Zinfandel, Syrah or Sauvignon Blanc

Ingredients
Chicken:
1 lb. orzo (rice shaped pasta)
15 oz. can mandarin oranges, drained
1 lb. seedless red grapes
8 green onions, sliced including tops
4 c. cooked shredded chicken breast
2 c. pineapple chunks, drained
1 c. slivered almonds, toasted

Dressing:
1/2 c. Consorzio Mango Vignette
1/3 c. Cucina Gio Extra Light Virgin Olive Oil
1 tsp. ground nutmeg
1 tsp. ground allspice
1/2 tsp. ground white pepper
1 tsp. salt

1/4 c. minced fresh cilantro
1/4 c. minced fresh mint

Directions

Prepare orzo according to package directions. Drain. Rinse under cool water; drain again. Place in a large bowl. Add oranges, grapes, green onions and chicken.

In a small bowl whisk together the Consorzio Mango Vignette, olive oil, nutmeg, allspice, salt and pepper. Stir in cilantro and mint. Pour over orzo-chicken mixture. Toss gently to coat. Chill before serving.

Place in serving dish and garnish with pineapple (2 c.) and almonds.

Kirsten Bushick

CHICKEN ITALIAN STYLE

Very popular and very easy.

Yield: 4 servings
Wine Suggestions: Sangiovese (Chanti), Merlot or Chardonnay.

Ingredients

1- 2 lb. fryer chicken, cut up
1 clove of garlic
4 tbsp. olive oil
salt
pepper
1 bay leaf
1/2 tsp. fresh basil
1/4 c. wine vinegar

Directions

Crush the garlic, brown gently in oil in a frying pan and then remove it. Rub salt and pepper on the chicken bits and brown it in the oil. Remove to a casserole dish and add the crushed herb and vinegar.

Cook slowly at 350 degrees for about 30 minutes.

Mrs. Cecily Littleton

Helpful Hints

A little oatmeal or quick-cooking oats add flavor and thickening to stew.
Grate a potato into a stew for a good thickener.

CHICKEN MARSALA

Serve with white and wild rice and a salad

Yield: 4 servings

Wine suggestions: Sangiovese (Chanti), Merlot, Chardonnay or Riesling.

Ingredients
6 chicken breasts, boned, skinned and cut in half
1/4 c. flour
3 tbsp. butter
1/4 c. minced onions
1 clove garlic, minced
1/2 lb. mushrooms, sliced
1/2 c. marsala wine
pepper (to taste)

Directions
Pound the chicken into thin cutlets between sheets of waxed paper. Mix flour with pepper (to taste). Dredge the chicken in flour.

In a large skillet, sauté the onions, garlic and mushrooms in butter (add a little vegetable oil to prevent burning). Sauté chicken for 2 - 3 minutes on each side. Add wine and reserved mushroom mixture. Cook until tender (about 3 minutes). Remove to heated platter. Bring pan juices to a boil and cook until it is a thin glaze. Pour over chicken.

Helen Lungren

CHRISTMAS CHICKEN

So called, since we always serve it on Christmas Eve. This can be made a day ahead, but if you do, reserve some sour cream and broth and add before reheating. If you fix the whole thing and decide to bake it on the next day, add all the sour cream just before baking.

Yield: 8 - 10 . But it can be made for up to 32, as you see below.

Wine Suggestions: Syrah, Merlot, Zinfandel or Chardonnay.

Ingredients

To serve		_32_	_8-10_	_10-14_
chicken breasts		12	4	8
water	c.	6	2	4
dry sherry	c.	3	1	2

To serve		32	8-10	10-14	
salt	tsp.	4 1/2	1 1/2	3	
curry powder	tsp.	1 1/2	1/2	1	
celery, diced	c.	1 1/2	1/2	1	
white onions		3	1	2	
mushrooms	lb.	3	1	2	
margarine	c.	3/4	1/4	1/2	
rice	pkgs.	3	2	1	*(Uncle Ben's long grained wild rice with seasonings)*
sour cream	c.	3	1	2	
creamed soups					
mushroom	cans	1	-	-	
celery	cans	1	1	2	
chicken	cans	1	-	-	

Directions

To the water, add the first 7 ingredients. Simmer until chicken is tender. Remove the chicken and allow to cool. Then remove the skin from the chicken and cut into bite-sized pieces.

Strain the broth and use it in place of the water needed to cook the rice (substitute broth for water according to the box instructions) .

Sauté the mushrooms in margarine until tender (do not drain). In a large bowl, combine the cooked chicken, rice, mushrooms with liquid, the sour cream and the undiluted cream soups. Blend well.

Pour into greased casserole and bake at 350 degrees for 45 - 60 minutes, until bubbly. Do not brown the top. Leftovers freeze well.

Richard Coyle

CLAIRE'S LEMON ROLL-UPS

Leftovers refrigerate well and can be reheated in the microwave. Flounder works very well in this recipe.

Yield: 8 servings. However, you might want to make more since our guests normally request seconds.

Wine Suggestions: Riesling, Chardonnay or Sauvignon Blanc

Ingredients

1/3 c. butter
1/3 c. reconstituted lemon juice
2 chicken bouillon cubes

1 tsp. Tabasco
1 c. cooked rice
1- 10 oz. pkg. frozen chopped broccoli, thawed
1 c. (4 oz.) shredded sharp cheese
8 fish fillets (about 2 lb.) fresh or frozen (thawed)

Directions

Preheat oven to 375 degrees. In a small saucepan melt butter. Then add lemon juice, bouillon and Tabasco. Heat slowly until the bouillon dissolves: set aside. In medium bowl combine: rice, broccoli, cheese and 1/4 cup of the lemon-butter sauce mixture, mixing well.

Divide the broccoli mixture evenly among the fillets. Roll up and place each seam side down in a shallow baking dish. Pour remaining sauce mixture over the roll-ups. Bake for 25 minutes or until the fish flakes with a fork.

Spoon sauce over each individual serving and garnish with paprika.

Claire Coyle

COCONUT CHICKEN

Serve this great chicken dish with white and wild rice and a green salad.

Yield: 4 - 6 servings. Quick and easy to prepare
Wine Suggestions: Pinot Noir, Riesling, Chardonnay or Zinfandel.

Ingredients

4 boneless chicken breasts, split
1/2 c. coconut
1/4 c. bread crumbs
1/4 c. butter, melted
salt and pepper to taste

Directions

Mix the bread crumbs and coconut together.

Dip the chicken in the butter and roll in the bread crumb and coconut mixture. Bake in a greased baking dish for 45 minutes at 375 degrees.

Do not turn the chicken over while it is baking.

Helen Lungren

COUSCOUS CHICKEN

Yield: 4 servings

Wine Suggestions: Zinfandel, Syrah, Merlot or Riesling

Ingredients

1 lb. boneless chicken breasts
1c. peas
3 oz. raisins (2 small boxes)
1/2 c. slivered blanched almonds
2 tbsp. butter
1 1/2 c. water
1 c. whole wheat couscous

Directions

Melt better in a medium-size, covered sauce pan. Add almonds and stir on medium heat as they brown. Cut chicken into bite size pieces. In non-stick skillet, stir fry the chicken. Then add the raisins and peas. Keep warm. When almonds are nicely browned, add 1 1/2 c. water. Bring to boil and add one cup of whole wheat couscous. Stir. Bring to a second boil, then cover and reduce heat. Simmer until couscous absorbs the liquid (about 2 minutes).

Remove from heat. Add chicken, peas and raisins. Stir to blend. Cover and let stand for 5 minutes. Add salt and pepper to taste.

Lynne Urian

CRAB CAKES

Yield: 4 servings

Wine Suggestions: Muscadet (French), Sauvignon Blanc, Pinot Gris, Riesling, Rose or Pinot Noir

Ingredients

1 lb. crabmeat
3/4 c. bread crumbs
1/4 c. chopped parsley
2 tbsp. chopped scallions
1/2 tsp. Worcestershire sauce
1 egg
Salt and pepper to taste

Directions

Mix all ingredients and chill in patties. Cook in butter on each side until brown. Serve with tartar sauce.

Helen Lungren

EASY BLACK BEAN LASAGNA

A hit at St. George's Lenten Wednesday suppers.

Yield: 10 servings

Wine Suggestions: Zinfandel, Sangiovese or California Chardonnay.

Ingredients

1 (15 oz.) can black beans, drained and rinsed
1 (28 oz.) can crushed tomatoes, undrained
3/4 c. onion, chopped
1/2 c. green pepper, chopped
1/2 c. chunky salsa
1 tsp. chili powder
1/2 tsp. cumin
1 c. light ricotta cheese
1/8 tsp. garlic power
1 egg
10 uncooked lasagna noodles
1 1/2 c. shredded cheddar or mozzarella cheese (6 oz.)

Directions

Heat oven to 350 degrees. Spray a 13 in. x 9 in. (3 qt.) baking dish with non-stick cooking spray. In a large bowl, mash beans slightly. Stir in tomatoes, onion, green pepper, salsa, chili powder and cumin. Mix well. In a small bowl, combine ricotta cheese, garlic powder and egg; blend well.

Spread 1 c. of the tomato mixture over the bottom of the spray-coated dish. Top with half of the noodles, overlapping slightly. Top with 1/2 of the remaining tomato mixture. Spoon ricotta mixture over top; spread carefully. Top with 1/2 of the cheese, then the rest of the noodles, tomato mixture and cheese.

Cover tightly with spray-coated foil.

Bake at 350 degrees for 40 - 45 minutes or until noodles are tender. Uncover; let stand 15 minutes before serving.

Terri McFarland

Helpful Hints

Instead of using a metal roasting rack, make a grid of celery and carrot sticks and place meat or poultry on it. The additional advantage - vegetables flavor the pan drippings

---

EASY LASAGNA

St. George's Cookbook of the past brings an all time favorite to the present

Yield: 6 - 8 servings

Wine Suggestions: Sangiovese/Chianti, Barbera, Barbaresco or Zinfandel

Ingredients

1 lb. hamburger
4 - 5 c. spaghetti sauce
8 oz. lasagna, uncooked
1 lb. Ricotta cheese
8 oz. shredded Mozzarella cheese
1 c. grated Parmesan cheese

Directions

Brown the hamburger and add spaghetti sauce. In a baking dish approximately 13 x 9 x 2 inches, spread about 1 cup of the sauce mixture. Arrange a layer of uncooked lasagna. Top with more sauce, Ricotta, Mozzarella, Parmesan and sauce. Repeat, gently pressing lasagna pieces into cheese mixture below it. Add final layer of lasagna. Pour remaining sauce over all, making sure all lasagna pieces are covered with sauce. Top with remaining Mozzarella and Parmesan.

Bake at 350 degrees for 45 - 55 minutes until it is lightly browned and bubbly. Allow to stand 15 minutes.

Mary Beumer

EGGPLANT PARMIGIANA

When eggplants are in season, this is a wonderful treat!

Yield: 6 servings

Wine Suggestions: Sangiovese (Chianti), Barbera, Merlot or Cabernet Sauvignon

Ingredients

1 medium eggplant
2 eggs, beaten
2 tbsp. water
3/4 c. dry bread crumbs
3/4 c. cooking oil
1/2 c. grated parmesan cheese
1 tsp. dried oregano leaves
1 tsp. dried basil leaves
1/2 tsp. salt

1/2 lb. mozzarella cheese,sliced
3 (8 oz.) cans tomato sauce

Directions

Peel the eggplant and cut it into 1/4 inch slices. Dip slices into mixture of beaten egg and water and then into bread crumbs. Brown on both sides in hot oil, removing the slices as they brown. Combine the grated parmesan cheese, oregano, basil and salt.

Place 1/3 of the cooked eggplant into a greased 2 qt. oval casserole dish. Sprinkle with 1/3 of the parmesan cheese mixture. Top with 1/3 of the mozzarella sliced cheese and 1 can of tomato sauce. Repeat these layers 2 times.

Bake in a 350 degree oven for 30 minutes or until the sauce is bubbly.

Mildred F. Burns

FISH BAKE

Use orange roughy, perch or haddock.

Yield: 4 servings

Wine Suggestions: Pinot Gris, French Chardonnay, Riesling, Muscadet or Sancerre (French).

Ingredients

1 lb. fish
1 can diced tomatoes
1 onion, sliced
1 green pepper, sliced
2 tbsp. butter or olive oil
lemon and pepper seasoning
Italian bread crumbs
Parmesan cheese

Directions

Oil a pan. Place tomatoes, onion and pepper in the pan. Place the fish upon the vegetable bed. Pour melted butter or olive oil over the fish.

Cover fish with as much of the bread crumbs as needed. Then add parmesan cheese over the bread crumbs.

Bake uncovered at 350 degrees for 25 minutes.

Richard Coyle

GERMAN APPLESAUCE MEAT LOAF

Very moist and tasty.

Yield: 6 - 8 servings
Wine Suggestions: Cabernet Sauvignon, Zinfandel, Syrah or Sangiovese.

Ingredients
vegetable oil
1 1/2 lbs. ground beef
1/2 lb. ground pork
1/2 c. finely diced onion
1 c. applesauce
1 c. bread crumbs
3 tbsp. catsup
2 tsp. salt
1/4 tsp. black pepper

Directions
Heat the oven to 350 degrees. Lightly oil a 9 x 5 loaf pan. Combine all ingredients and mix well. Place in the prepared pan. Bake till the juices run clear, about 1 1/2 - 2 hours. Cool in the pan on a wire rack for about 10-15 minutes. Then turn out on a platter and slice and serve.

Dolores Jaquith

GRATED ZUCCHINI PENNE

A quick, easy and delicious meal.

Yield: 4 - 6 servings
Wine Suggestions: Zinfandel, Merlot, Sangiovese, Riesling or Sauvignon Blanc.

Ingredients
5 medium zucchini
1 lb. penne pasta
3 tbsp. olive oil
2 garlic cloves, minced
1 c. grated cheese
a pinch or red pepper flakes (optional)

Directions
Fill a 6 qt. pot with water and heat to a boil. While water boils, clean and grate zucchini in a colander. Allow to drain. When water boils throw in the pasta and cook according to box directions.

At the same time heat 3 tbsp. olive oil in a 6 qt. pot, add grated zucchini and cook for approximately 5 minutes over a medium-high heat. Stir frequently. Add the 2 garlic cloves, stirring constantly for 1 - 2 minutes. Add the red pepper flakes for a zing and continue cooking and stirring. When the pasta is just about done, add 1 cup grated cheese to the zucchini and stir until it is well mixed.

Drain the pasta. Then stir in the zucchini mixture. Have additional grated cheese available for sprinkling on the pasta.

Robin D. Monteleone

GRILLED BUTTERFLY LEG OF LAMB

Great to serve to people who really don't like lamb.

Yield: 6 - 8 servings
Wine Suggestions: Cabernet Sauvignon, Syrah, Sangiovese or Zinfandel.

Ingredients
1 butterflied leg of lamb

Marinade:
2 tbsp. red pepper (crushed)
1 c. lemon juice (Real Lemon works well)
3/4 c. olive oil
8 small shallots, chopped
2 garlic cloves, crushed
2 tsp. fresh ground pepper
2 tsp. coriander
1/2 c. wine (white or red)

Directions
Have the butcher butterfly the leg of lamb and remove as much fat as possible. Usually you will have to remove excess fat from the lamb yourself. It is very important to do this step.

Mix all marinade ingredients together and marinate the lamb overnight, if possible, or at least 4 - 5 hours.

Grill on medium heat (350 degrees) for 45 - 60 minutes. I like to serve it slightly pink with peppercorn gravy.

Richard Coyle

LEMON CHICKEN BREASTS

A recipe from the Reverend Alan Salmon of Christ Church in Riverton, NJ

Yield: 6 - 8 servings. Prepare the day before serving.
Wine Suggestions: Merlot, Pinot Noir, Riesling or Chardonnay

Ingredients
6 whole chicken breasts, halved, skinned and boned
2 c. sour cream
1/4 c. lemon juice
1 clove crushed garlic
4 tsp. celery salt
2 tsp. paprika
1/2 tsp. pepper
1/4 c. melted butter
1/2 c. oil (not olive oil)
1/4 c. bread crumbs

Directions
Mix sour cream, lemon juice, garlic and seasonings. Add chicken breast and refrigerate overnight. The next day, roll the chicken breasts in the bread crumbs and place them in a greased shallow pan. Melt the butter and oil and spoon it over the chicken.

Bake for 45 minutes in a 350 degree oven.

Helen Lungren

LINGUINE DUE PESCE

Tuna noodle dinner for real grown-ups. Only 15 minutes to prepare!

Yield: 4 servings
Wine Suggestions: Sangiovese, Syrah, Zinfandel or Chardonnay.

Ingredients
1 lb. linguine
1 can white tuna fish
1 can flat anchovy fillets, deboned and soaked in warm water
1 tbsp. butter
15 pitted black olives, sliced
3 spring onions and stalks, sliced
1 tsp. capers

1 tsp. parsley
1 c. heavy cream
salt
pepper

Directions

Start the linguine. While it is cooking, gently melt butter in a frying pan. Break up the tuna into pieces and add to the butter. Then add the black olives, spring onions, capers, parsley and salt and pepper to taste. Take the deboned anchovies, cut them in squares and add them to the tuna. Heat all the ingredients gently until soft and cooked down, about 5 minutes. Turn off the heat. Add the cream. Now, it will be too wet, so gently cook and stir until the cream boils down, about 5 minutes.

Finish cooking the linguine and drain. Serve on plates with the sauce on top.

Mrs. Cecily Littleton

LINGUINE WITH TOMATOES AND JALAPENOS

This is a recipe for people who like extra spice in their lives, like the Turco Family of The Children's Ark. It's a fun dish to build a dinner around and the leftovers, if there are any, can be served chilled as a quick and easy side dish. Don't tell anyone that this is a healthy, low-fat recipe!

Yield: 4 servings
Wine Suggestions: Syrah, Sangiovese, Sauvignon Blanc or Zinfandel.

Ingredients

1 whole head of garlic
1 tsp. olive oil
3 tbsp. finely chopped jalapeno pepper
3 c. chopped plum tomatoes
3 c. hot cooked linguine (about 6 oz. uncooked)
1 c. (4 oz.) grated fresh Parmesan cheese, divided
3 tbsp. chopped fresh oregano
2 tbsp. fresh lemon juice
1 tbsp. anchovy paste
1/4 tsp. freshly ground pepper

Directions

Preheat oven to 350 degrees. Remove white papery skin from garlic (don't peel or separate cloves). Wrap garlic head in foil. Bake at 350 degrees for 1 hour; let cool 10 minutes. Separate cloves, squeeze to extract garlic pulp. Discard skins.

Heat oil in a non-stick skillet over medium-high heat. Add jalapeno pepper and sauté for 30 seconds. Add tomato and sauté for 2 minutes. Remove skillet from heat and stir in garlic pulp. Add pasta, 1/2 cup cheese, oregano, and next 3 ingredients. Toss well.

Sprinkle each serving with remaining cheese and additional pepper if desired.

Stefanie Turco

MACARONI AND CHEESE

The best macaroni and cheese ever.

Yield: 12 servings. Can be easily divided in half.

Wine Suggestions: Sangiovese (Chianti), Barbera/Barberesco (Italian), Syrah, Cabernet Sauvignon or Riesling.

Ingredients
8 tbsp. unsalted butter (plus more to butter the dish)
6 slices white bread - crusts removed and broken into 1/4 - 1/2 inch pieces
5 1/2 c. milk
1/2 c. of all purpose flour
2 tsp. salt
1/4 tsp. nutmeg
1/4 tsp. ground black pepper
1/4 tsp. cayenne pepper
4 1/2 c. grated sharp white cheddar cheese
2 c. grated Gruyère or 1 1/4 c. grated Pecorino Romano cheese
1 lb. elbow macaroni

Directions
Heat the oven to 375 degrees. Butter a 3 qt. casserole and place the bread pieces in a bowl. Melt 2 tbsp. butter, add to bread, toss and set aside. In medium saucepan melt 6 tbsp. butter over medium heat. When the butter bubbles, add flour and then stir and cook for 1 minute.

Slowly pour in heated milk and whisk until mixture becomes thick and bubbles. Remove from heat. Stir in salt, pepper, nutmeg, cayenne, cheddar cheese and 2 c. Gruyère (or 1 1/4 c. Pecorino Romano cheese). Set aside.

Cook macaroni but do not over cook it. Drain and rinse the macaroni with cold water. Drain well. Stir macaroni into cheese sauce. Pour into prepared dish and sprinkle remaining cheeses over the top. Scatter the bread pieces on the top.

Bake until browned for about 30 minutes. Transfer to rack, cool for 5 minutes and serve.

Elizabeth Edwards

MARINATED BEEF KABOBS

One of our family favorites, especially when cooked on the grill.

Yield: approximately 8 kabobs

Wine Suggestions: Zinfandel, Merlot, Cabernet Sauvignon or Syrah.

Ingredients

Kabobs:
1 lb. top round beef steak, 3/4 inch thick
12 whole medium mushrooms
1 large red bell pepper, cut into 12 pieces
1 zucchini or yellow summer squash, sliced
approximately 8 skewers

Marinade:
1/4 c. chopped green onions
2 tbsp. sugar
2 tbsp. sesame seed
2 tbsp. oil
1 tbsp. vinegar
1 tsp. grated ginger root or 1/4 tsp. ginger
1 garlic clove, minced

Directions

Cut steak into 1/4 inch strips. Combine all marinade ingredients in a nonmetal bowl or resealable plastic bag. Add steak to marinade and toss to coat. Cover bowl or seal in a bag and refrigerate 6 hours or overnight. Remove steak, reserving marinade. Thread steak strips onto skewers, alternating with vegetables.

Cook on gas grill over medium heat or on a charcoal grill 4 - 6 inches from the coals for about 10 - 15 minutes or until desired doneness. Turn and brush with reserved marinade. Alternatively, you can broil in the oven, 4 - 6 inches from the heat for about 5 - 10 minutes.

The Lee Family

MEATBALL STEW IN THE SLO COOKER

Yield: 6 servings

Wine Suggestions: Sangiovese, Barbera, Syrah, Zinfandel or Cabernet Sauvignon.

Ingredients

3 medium potatoes, peeled and diced

1 pkg. baby carrots cut into quarters
1 large onion, chopped
3 celery stalks, sliced
1 pkg. frozen cooked meatballs
1 can tomato condensed soup (10 3/4 oz.)
1 can beef gravy
1 c. water
1 envelope onion soup mix
2 tsp. or 2 cubes of beef bullion

Directions
Place the potatoes, carrots, onions, celery and the meatballs in a 5 qt. slo cooker. In a bowl combine the remaining ingredients and pour over meatball mixture. Cover and cook on low for 9 - 10 hours or till the vegetables are done.

Dolores Jaquith

MINCEMEAT - THE REAL THING

This "blast from the past" was in the old St. George's Cookbook. Try it this holiday.

Yield: 4 large pies
Wine Suggestions: Merlot, Syrah or Zinfandel

Ingredients
1 lb. lean beef, cooked and cooled
1/2 lb. suet
1 orange, rind and juice
2 1/2 lb. apples, peeled and cored
1 lb. seeded raisins
1 lb. seedless raisins
1/2 lb. currants (optional)
3/8 lb. citron, cut fine
1 tbsp. each of cinnamon, nutmeg and mace
1 tbsp. each of cloves, allspice and salt
1 1/4 lb. brown sugar
1 pint grape juice
1 c. weak cider vinegar

Directions
Put beef, suet and orange through a food grinder using the finest blade. Then, grind the apples using a medium blade. Mix all the ingredients together thoroughly. Allow to blend at least 10 days in the refrigerator before using or freezing.

This recipe freezes well and makes almost a gallon.

Shirley Norton

MOM'S SUNDAY SPAGHETTI GRAVY

Every Sunday, my mom, Eve D'Augostino, would get up before church and make gravy. Dad would buy Italian bread and by the time we got home the gravy was ready for dipping. After I was married and returned home for Christmas dinner and other holidays, I swear I could smell the gravy coming out of the kitchen as soon as I hit the sidewalk. Thanks Mom!

Yield: enough for a large Italian family. The recipe below indicates everything that could possible go into gravy, meatballs, sausage, braciole and pork. This was used for big family holidays. Regular weekly gravy may include just meatballs and pork ribs or another combination. However, the best gravy always includes both a beef and a pork.
Wine Suggestions: Sangiovese (Chianti), Zinfandel, Barolo or Barbera.

Ingredients
Gravy:
1/3 c. olive oil
1 medium onion, peeled and whole
2 cloves of garlic, whole
1 lb. pork, meaty country ribs work well
3/4 lb. sweet Italian sausage cut into 2 1/2 inch pieces
3 - 4 cans peeled, crushed tomatoes (1 lb. and 12 oz. cans). I like Pastene or San Marzano
2 - 3 cups of water
1 1/2 - 2 tbsp. salt
1 - 1 1/2 tsp. black pepper
several sprigs each of fresh basil, oregano and parsley, finely chopped together.

Meatballs:
2 lb. ground beef
2 eggs
1 small onion, minced
2 sprigs chopped parsley
2/3 c. seasoned bread crumbs
1/3 c. grated cheese. Loccatelli preferred.
Combine all ingredients and form into meatballs. This will make about 15 of them.

Brachiole:
1/2 lb. beef prepared as scallopini (pounded 1/4 inch thick and cut into approx. 3 x 4 inch pieces)
1/2 small onion, minced
few sprigs of fresh parsley, finely chopped
salt and pepper to taste
Lay out beef. Sprinkle each piece with minced onion, parsley, salt and pepper. Roll up and secure with string or long toothpicks. Make sure to remove these before serving.

Directions

Make meatballs and braciole following the recipe previously described. Then, heat oil in a large heavy-bottomed pot. Brown onion and garlic then remove them from the oil. Brown pork, sausages, braciole and meatballs in hot oil until brown on all sides. (This will need to be done in batches)

When all meat is browned and removed from the pot, put in the crushed tomatoes, oregano, basil and parsley. Add salt and pepper to taste. Add water to desired consistency. Bring the partially covered pot to a low simmer and cook for 1 1/2 hour.

This can be separated into batches and frozen for a few meals.

Donna DiPaulo

PAELLA CON POLLO

An easy, tasty chicken dish.

Yield: 6 servings

Wine Suggestions: Chardonnay, Riesling, Merlot, Zinfandel or Syrah.

Ingredients

4 chicken breasts
1/2 c. olive oil
2 c. uncooked rice
1/8 tsp. minced garlic
1/4 tsp. saffron
4 c. chicken broth
1 tsp. salt
1 c. cooked ham
2- 4 1/2 oz. cans shrimp
1 can clams
1/2 c. onion, chopped

Directions

Cut the chicken into small pieces and cook in oil until brown. Remove from heat. Brown the rice, onion, garlic and saffron in the remaining oil. Add chicken, broth, salt, ham, shrimp and clams. Cook until rice is fluffy and chicken is done.

From the previous St. George's Cookbook

Helpful Hints

With knife make small holes in pork chops or roast. Cut garlic and put in holes. Season as usual.

PEANUT NOODLES WITH CHICKEN AND PEARS

A quick, easy recipe when you're in the mood for chicken.

Yield: 8 servings

Wine Suggestions: Pinot Grigio, Syrah, Zinfandel or Gewurztraminer (Alsace/German)

Ingredients
1 lb. spaghetti
1 c. smooth peanut butter
1 c. water, at room temperature
1/4 c. white vinegar
1 tbsp. sesame oil
2 tsp. kosher salt
1/2 precooked roasted chicken, shredded (2 cups)
1 Asian or Bosc pear, peeled and thinly sliced
5 scallions, trimmed and thinly sliced
1/3 c. roasted peanuts, roughly chopped
3 small red serrano chilies, thinly sliced (optional)

Directions
Cook the spaghetti al dente according to the package instructions. Drain, rinse with cold water, then drain again. Combine peanut butter, water, vinegar, oil and salt to make a smooth sauce. Toss the noodles with the peanut sauce. Arrange on a platter and top with the chicken, pear, scallions, peanuts and chilies.

To make ahead:
Mix the sauce and cook the spaghetti up to 1 day beforehand. Refrigerate separately. Bring sauce to room temperature before mixing with pasta.

Kirsten Bushick

PHARSALIA CASSEROLE

A great dish from my hometown, Lynchburg, VA.

Yield: 8 - 10 servings

Wine Suggestions: Zinfandel, Merlot or Sangiovese.

Ingredients
8 oz. cream cheese
2 c. sour cream

1 tsp. salt
1/2 tsp. pepper
3 chopped medium onions
1 1/2 lb. lean ground beef
2 tbsp. butter
2- 8 oz. cans tomato sauce
1 tbsp. sugar
1 tsp. Worcestershire sauce
2- 5 oz. pkgs. thin egg noodles
1/2 c. shredded cheddar cheese

Directions

Mix together cream cheese, sour cream, salt, pepper and onions. Set aside. Brown ground beef in butter; add tomato sauce, sugar and Worcestershire sauce. Cook noodles according to directions. Put half of the noodles on the bottom of a greased 2 qt. casserole dish. Top with half of the meat mixture, then half of the cheese mixture. Repeat the layers. Top with cheddar cheese.

Bake in preheated 350 degree oven until hot and browned, about 30 minutes.

Jennifer Robelo

PIZZA TOT CASSEROLE

A big success at covered dish brunches

Yield: 6 - 8 servings

Wine Suggestions: Sangiovese (Chianti), Zinfandel or Syrah.

Ingredients

1 lb. ground beef
1 medium green pepper, chopped
1 medium onion, chopped
2 jars of pizza sauce
1- 4 1/2 oz. jar of sliced mushrooms, drained
2 c. (8 oz.) of mozzarella cheese
1 pkg. of frozen tater tots

Directions

In a skillet cook the beef, green pepper and onion until meat is no longer pink. Drain. Add sauce and mushrooms. Transfer to a 13 x 9 x 2 baking dish. Top with the cheese and potatoes. Bake uncovered at 400 degrees for 30 - 35 minutes or until golden brown.

Dolores Jacquith

POACHED SALMON

Yield: 4 servings

Wine Suggestions: Pinot Noir, Pinot Gris (Oregon), Riesling or Chardonnay.

Ingredients

1 onion, coarsely chopped
1/4 c. coarsely chopped celery
1 c. dry white wine
2 c. water
4- 6 oz. salmon fillets
Mustard Sauce
1/2 c. sour cream
1/2 c. plain yogurt
1 tbsp. Dijon mustard
3 dashes hot red pepper sauce
2 tsp. fresh dill
1/2 tsp. salt
salmon caviar and dill sprigs for garnish

Directions

In a skillet, combine vegetables, wine and water. Heat to simmering. Add salmon and poach for 4 minutes, covered, till the salmon feels firm yet springy. Combine sauce ingredients.

Arrange salmon on plates, spoon sauce on top and garnish with caviar and dill.

Elizabeth Edwards

POACHED SALMON

May be served hot or at room temperature. Great for party buffets.

Yield: Number of servings depends on the size of the salmon filet.

Wine Suggestions: Pinot Noir, Pinot Gris or Riesling.

Ingredients

salmon filet
powdered garlic
dried chives
butter buds sprinkles
paprika (ground)
white wine

Directions

Place the salmon in a shallow baking pan. Size depends on the size of the salmon. Sprinkle salmon with powdered garlic, butter buds, dried chives and paprika, in that order. Add enough white wine to cover the bottom of the pan.

Cover pan with foil and place in a 350 degree oven for 20-40 minutes, depending on the size of the fillet. Cook until salmon flakes.

Place salmon on a tray on a bed of lettuce leaves. Garnish with pimento and fresh parsley or dill.

Richard Coyle

PORK TENDERLOIN WITH MOROCCAN SPICES

This is great prepared ahead. Because of the short roasting time it can be popped into the oven just before serving the first course. It is good cold as well.

Yield: 6 servings

Wine Suggestions: Merlot, Zinfandel or Syrah

Ingredients

2 pork tenderloins
4 - 5 slices of bacon per loin

Blend together the following spices:
2 tsp. salt
1/2 tsp. pepper
1 tbsp. cumin
2 tsp. paprika
2 tsp. ground ginger
1 tsp. cinnamon
1 tsp. ground coriander

Directions

Wrap bacon in a spiral fashion around the length of the tenderloins, overlapping the ends and securing with toothpicks.

Tear a strip of wax paper or plastic wrap the length of the tenderloin. Sprinkle half of the spice mix on the paper and roll meat until bacon is coated. Repeat with the second loin.

Bake until the bacon is golden and crisp. About 30 minutes at 350 degrees. Let meat set for 5 minutes before slicing. Remove toothpicks as the meat is sliced.

Bryn Thompson

ROAST BARBECUE

A favorite of Chris Smythe's, especially on a winter Saturday afternoon.

Yield: 12 servings
Wine Suggestions: Cabernet Sauvignon, Syrah or Zinfandel.

Ingredients
3 lbs. chuck roast
2 tbsp. shortening
1 large onion, chopped
2 tbsp. vinegar
2 tbsp. lemon juice
3/4 c. water
1/2 c. cup chopped celery
2 c. catsup
3 tbsp. Worcestershire sauce
2 tbsp. brown sugar
1 tbsp. prepared mustard
2 tbsp. chili powder
1 tsp. salt
1/4 tsp. pepper

Directions
Trim meat and brown in shortening. Add the remaining ingredients. Bring to a boil; reduce heat to low. When the meat is tender enough (after approximately 2 - 3 hours), use two forks and shred or pull the meat apart. Continue cooking the meat until it is very tender (the time involved in this step is approximately 3 - 6 hours).

Serve on buns.

Bryn Smythe

ROASTED SALMON

This was an entree at the St. George's 2003 Progressive Dinner.

Yield: 6 servings
Wine Suggestions: Pinot Gris, Pinot Noir, Riesling or Chardonnay

Ingredients
1/3 c. dry white wine
1/3 c. orange juice

1/3 c. soy sauce
6- 6 oz. salmon fillets with skin

Directions

Mix wine, soy sauce and juice in a 13 x 9 x 2 inch glass baking dish. Place salmon, flesh side down, in the dish. Cover with plastic wrap and refrigerate 2 hours, turning occasionally.

Preheat oven to 450 degrees. Line baking sheet with foil. Shake excess marinade from salmon. Transfer salmon to baking sheet, skin side down. Roast until salmon is opaque in the center, about 14 minutes.

Sprinkle with salt. Transfer to plates.

Terry McFarland

ROTELLANI

Yield: makes 10 rotellanis
Wine Suggestions: Sangiovese, Syrah or Cabernet Sauvignon

Ingredients
2 lb. veal or beef shoulder, trimmed
2 c. seasoned breadcrumbs
1 c. olive oil
1 lb. bacon, cooked and chopped
1 lb. prosciutto, chopped
1 lb. spinach, cooked and chopped
1 lb. American cheese, shredded

Directions

From the shoulder roast, cut beef or veal into 1/4 in. slices to make a cutlet. Pound out with a tenderizing mallet. Brush and bread both sides with olive oil and seasoned breadcrumbs.

Place on the center end (so that the meat is longer in width than height), crumble bacon, American cheese, prosciutto and spinach. Add garlic and season to taste.

Close flaps on left and right over filling and then roll them up.

Place 4 - 5 on a metal skewer with a bay leaf between each. Grill over medium heat for 20 minutes turning occasionally.

Pete Ricci

RUMP ROAST LEFT OVERS

This is a favorite at the Waters' house. Roast the beef the night before and take it to the market and ask them to slice it thin.

Eat your meal and then use the leftovers for this recipe.

Yield: about 20 servings

Wine suggestions: Cabernet Sauvignon, Merlot, Zinfandel, or Syrah.

Ingredients

4 c. of 2 inch strips of cooked rump roast
1/4 c. vinegar
1 1/2 c. water
1/4 c. granulated sugar
4 tsp. prepared mustard
1/2 c. butter
2 sliced medium onions
1/4 tsp. pepper
1 tbsp. salt (or to taste)
1/4 tsp. cayenne pepper
2 thick lemon slices
1 c. catsup or chili sauce
3 tbsp. Worcestershire sauce
celery sliced on an angle
pitted ripe olives (optional)
about 20 hamburger rolls

Directions

Combine the vinegar and the next 9 ingredients and simmer the mixture uncovered for 20 minutes in a skillet. Then, add catsup or chili sauce, Worcestershire and the leftover meat. Refrigerate the mixture.

Approximately 45 minutes before eating, return the beef to simmer slowly until it is heated through. Sprinkle the top with celery and olives.

To serve, spoon the beef between split, toasted hamburger buns.

Anne Waters

Helpful Hints

Chopped toasted almonds add a pleasant crunchiness and make an attractive garnish for fish.

SALMON CAKES

My mother-in-law gave me this recipe shortly after we were married and it's still one of our favorite dinners.

Yield: 4 servings

Wine Suggestions: Pinot Gris, Sauvignon Blanc, Chardonnay or Riesling.

Ingredients
1- 14 3/4 oz. can red salmon
1/2 c. bread crumbs
1/2 c. onion
1 beaten egg
1/2 c. lemon juice
1/4 tsp. salt and pepper
additional 1/2 c. bread crumbs

Tartar Sauce:
3/4 c. mayonnaise
1/4 c. pickle relish (drained)
2 tbsp. chopped onion
1 tbsp. chopped parsley

Directions
Drain salmon, flake and remove the skin and bones.

Pour lemon juice over salmon and marinate in the refrigerator (covered) for 1 hour.

Add remaining ingredients and make into patties. Dip into bread crumbs and fry in Crisco about 5 minutes on each side. Drain and serve with tartar sauce.

To make the tartar sauce, mix together all the ingredients. Cover and chill for at least 2 hours. Makes one cup.

I serve this with macaroni and cheese and stewed tomatoes.

Helen Lungren

Helpful Hints

With knife make small holes in pork chops or roast. Cut garlic and put in holes. Season as usual.

SALMON LOAF

This can be eaten cold with salad or in a sandwich.

Yield: 4 servings
Wine Suggestions: Pinot Noir, Riesling or Chardonnay.

Ingredients
1 large tin of pink salmon
1 can of tomato soup (10 3/4 oz.)
1 3/4 c. fresh white bread crumbs
2 tbsp. chopped red pepper
2 tbsp. chopped sweet relish
2 eggs beaten with a little water

Directions
Unroll salmon and remove the black skin. Mix all ingredients together until well mixed. Grease a 9 x 5 inch loaf pan and pack in the mixture. Heat the oven to 350 degrees and bake uncovered for 45 minutes.

Slice and serve with or without a favorite sauce.

Kate Gibbons

SAUERKRAUT AND PORK

A New Year's Day tradition in my family. Even people who do not usually like sauerkraut come back for seconds.

Yield: 6 - 8 servings. Serve with boiled red potatoes, mustard and your favorite bread
Wine Suggestions: Zinfandel, Merlot or Syrah

Ingredients
2 lbs. sauerkraut
3 medium onions
2 tbsp. bacon or pork fat
2 tart apples (peeled, cored and chopped)
6 slices cooked ham
6 smoked pork chops
6 franks or knockwurst
12 link sausages
6 peppercorns
1/4 c. gin
2 1/2 c. white wine

Directions

Soak sauerkraut in cold water for 15 minutes to remove brine. To do this you can place in a colander and run water over it. Sauté onions in fat, add sauerkraut toss with fork and cook for 5 minutes stirring occasionally. Add apples, peppercorns and gin. Stir. Now add white wine and cook slowly covered for 1 hour.

Meanwhile, fry sausage, drain and soak on paper towel. Add other meats to the sauerkraut and cook covered for 30 minutes. Discard peppercorns before serving.

Karen Schloesser

SEA SCALLOPS AND ORANGE CREME SAUCE

I serve this dish over shell shaped pasta and with a side of bright green, steamed snow peas.

Yield: 4 - 6 servings
Wine Suggestions: Riesling, Pinot Gris/Grigio, or Muscadet (French) or Chardonnay

Ingredients
1 lb. sea scallops
1/2 c. flour
zest of 1 orange
2 tbsp. olive oil
juice from 1 orange
1/2 c. white wine
1/2 c. additional orange juice
2/3 c. cream
salt and pepper to taste

Directions

Heat oil over medium heat in a non-stick skillet. Add orange zest and cook for a minute or two to flavor the oil. Dredge the sea scallops lightly in flour. Add to pan and cook until golden brown. Turn scallops over and add juice from 1 orange and simmer scallops until cooked through to taste. Remove scallops and keep warm. To pan add additional 1/2 c. orange juice and 1/2 c. wine. Increase heat and stir until liquids reduce by about a half. Add 2/3 c. cream and cook and stir until sauce thickens.

Return scallops to pan and toss to coat. Salt and pepper to taste.

If your cardiologist isn't looking, a tbsp. or two of butter swirled in the sauce at the last minute adds a wonderful richness.

Lynne Urian

SEARED FLANK STEAK

Chris Smythe often prepared the steak ahead and served it cold with salsa to make a wonderful sandwich.

Yield: 4 servings
Wine Suggestions: Cabernet Sauvignon, Zinfandel or Sangiovese.

Ingredients
2/3 c. flat-leaf parsley leaves
1 garlic clove, minced
6 anchovy fillets
2 tbsp. drained capers
1 tsp. red wine vinegar
1/2 c. plus 1 tbsp. extra-virgin olive oil
1 lb. flank steak

Directions
In a food processor or blender, pulse the parsley, garlic, anchovies, capers and vinegar until coarsely chopped. With the machine on, slowly pour in 1/2 cup of the oil and mix just until blended.

In a large non-stick skillet, heat the remaining 1 tbsp. of oil until almost smoking. Season the steak and add it to the skillet. Cook the steak over moderately high heat until well seared outside and pink inside (approximately 5-6 minutes per side for medium rare).

Transfer to a cutting board and let stand for 5 minutes. Carve the steak across the grain into thin slices. Serve with salsa .

Bryn Smythe

SHREDDED PORK IN THE CROCK POT

Yield: 4 - 6 servings
Wine Suggestions: Zinfandel or Syrah.

Ingredients
3 lb. pork shoulder or boneless country ribs
6 - 10 garlic cloves
1 medium onion
Salt and pepper to taste
barbecue sauce
seasoned salt

Directions

Put the pork in the crock pot. Season with salt and pepper and put in about 6 - 10 cloves of garlic roughly chopped and the onion sliced into pieces. Add 1/2 cup of any kind of barbecue sauce and cook on low for about 6-8 hours.

When it is done take the pork and start to pull it apart with a fork until it is shredded. Add seasoned salt to taste and some more barbecue sauce, using a little bit or a lot depending on how wet you like the pork.

Serve on buns.

Liz Havens

SOUTHWESTERN SHRIMP CREOLE

Complete sauce may be made ahead. If you do this then reheat before serving and add shrimp and simmer until done (approximately 5 minutes). Stirring often.

Yield: 4 servings
Wine Suggestions: Chardonnay, Sangiovese or Sauvignon Blanc.

Ingredients
1 medium onion, chopped
1 large green pepper, chopped
2 cloves garlic, minced
1- 15 oz. can diced tomatoes with green chilies or 1 can (15 oz.) diced tomatoes and 1 tbsp. of diced chilies
1 tbsp. cooking oil
1/4 tsp. salt
1/4 tsp. pepper
1 small jar diced pimientos
1 lb. deveined and shelled shrimp
1 box of rice with or without green onions

Directions
In skillet place the oil and sauté the onion, pepper and garlic until it is tender. Over low heat, stir in pimientos, tomatoes, chilies, salt and pepper. Simmer for 10 minutes.

Add shrimp and simmer over low heat until done (approximately 5 minutes), stirring occasionally.

Serve over cooked rice.

Kate Gibbons

SPICY GARLIC SHRIMP ON WILTED GREENS

Another favorite at one of the "St. George's Men Cook" evenings.

Yield: 4 main course servings or 6 - 8 first course servings

Wine Suggestions: Gewurztraminer (Alsace/German/Washington State), Pinot Gris, or Chardonnay.

Ingredients

Shrimp:
1 lb. large shrimp, tail on, peeled and deveined
3 cloves garlic, chopped
1 oz. brandy
4 oz. dry white wine
juice of 1 lemon
3 tbsp. oil
2 tbsp. butter
red peppers, fresh ginger, scallions, salt and white pepper (to taste)

Sauce:
1/2 c. sugar
2 tbsp. light soy sauce
1/4 c. mango puree
1 tbsp. dark rum
1 tbsp. fresh lime juice

Greens:
1 tbsp. sherry
1 tbsp. light soy sauce
1 tsp. sugar
8 c. mixed spring greens and spinach, loosely packed
1/2 c. cilantro or basil, chopped
mango slices, for garnish

Directions

Shrimp:
Marinate shrimp, a few hours or overnight, in a mixture of wine, lemon juice, red pepper, chopped garlic, 1 tbsp. oil, salt and white pepper (to taste).

Heat a no-stick wok with 2 tbsp. oil and 2 tbsp. butter. Add scallions and ginger. Add shrimp and cook for one minute.

Add the brandy and flambe. Stir and cook for 2 minutes.

Sauce:
Remove all but 2 tbsp. of oil from the wok. Add the sauce ingredients and stir until the mixture bubbles. Return the shrimp to the wok and stir to coat with the sauce for a minute or two.

Transfer to holding container and keep warm.

Greens:
Heat 2 tbsp. of oil in the wok, add the sherry, soy sauce and sugar and stir to heat through. Add the greens/spinach mixture and stir briskly at high heat just until wilted. Remove from the heat, fold in cilantro/basil and transfer to serving platter.

Place the shrimp on the greens and garnish with mango slices.

Chris Smythe

STEAK ALLA PIZZAIOLO (TOMATOES AND OREGANO)

This is an economical main course which uses less expensive cuts of beef. It has its origins in Naples, Italy and has been handed down from my father's family. This dish goes well with boiled potatoes, a green vegetable and lots of Italian bread for sopping up the sauce.

Yield: 6 - 8 servings.
Wine Suggestions: Cabernet Sauvignon, Syrah or Barolo.

Ingredients
2 1/2 lbs. chuck or blade steak
1/4 c. olive oil
3 cloves garlic, crushed
2 lbs. ripe tomatoes, chopped or use 1- 1lb. 12 oz. can diced tomatoes
3 or 4 sprigs fresh oregano or 1 tbsp. dried
salt and pepper to taste
1/2 c. dry white wine (optional)

Directions
Heat oil in a large frying pan. Lightly brown garlic and steak on both sides. Add tomatoes, oregano, salt, pepper and wine.

Bring to a boil, reduce heat and simmer for 35 - 45 minutes until meat is tender.

Remove from the pan and slice and arrange on platter with the tomatoes.

Cynthia Pound

STUFFED FLANK STEAK

A recipe from the previous St. George's Cookbook

Yield: 2 - 4 servings, depending on the size of the steak
Wine Suggestions: Cabernet Sauvignon, Merlot, Zinfandel or Syrah

Ingredients
1- 2 lb. flank steak
1/2 bag of prepared stuffing
1 egg
onion salt
salt and pepper to taste

Directions
Prepare meat using a tenderizer. Moisten 1/2 bag of stuffing with an egg and a little water. Add onion salt, salt and pepper to season the mixture. Place the filling on the meat so that is it about 1/2 inch thick. Roll the meat like a jelly roll and tie it in 2 places.

Place in a baking dish about 1/2 filled with water and cover tightly with aluminum foil. Bake in 350 degree oven for 1 1/2 - 2 hours.

Serve with gravy, if desired.

Mary Beumer

STUFFED HOT DOGS

This is an easy and quick recipe handed down from my grandmother to us. Then it was passed to my children who have shared it with their friends.

Yield: the number of servings will depend on how much of each ingredient you use.
Wine Suggestions: Zinfandel or Syrah.

Ingredients
hot dogs
mashed potatoes
yellow American or Velveeta cheese

Directions
Preheat the oven to 350 degrees. Split each hot dog down the center. Stuff with mashed potatoes and cover with strips of cheese. Place on a cookie sheet and cook in the 350 degree oven for 20 minutes or until the cheese melts and the hot dogs are done.

Liz Havens

TOM CONNER'S BEER-BRAISED BEEF SHORT RIBS WITH SPICY MOLASSES MOP

This recipe was given to me by a dear friend and former congregant. A great cook, party animal and stained glass artist. A mop is a thin basting sauce, in this case a slightly sweet and spicy blend of molasses and hot pepper sauce.

Succulent, meaty beef short ribs take a fair amount of cooking time to reach optimum tenderness, but that step can be done days ahead. A brief, ten-minute finish over a smoky fire, or under an oven broiler, then heats and crisps the ribs, while the mop glazes them a rich brown. A nice horseradish sauce compliments these ribs.

Yield: 6 servings

Wine Suggestions: Zinfandel, Merlot, Cabernet Sauvignon or Syrah.

Ingredients

The Ribs:
5 lbs. beef short ribs, surface fat trimmed
3 1/2 c. (2 cans) beef broth
1- 12 oz. bottle, dark beer
1 medium onion, sliced
1 tsp. salt
1/2 tsp. dried thyme, crumbled

The Mop:
1/4 c. of the braising liquid
1/4 c. unsulfured molasses
2 tbsp. balsamic vinegar
2 1/2 tsp. hot pepper sauce (such as Tabasco)
1 tsp. salt

Directions

Preheat oven to 350 degrees. Combine the six rib ingredients in heavy large Dutch oven (or other heavy ovenproof pot). Bring to boil over medium heat. Cover and bake until ribs are very tender, turning occasionally, about 2 hours 50 minutes. Cover and refrigerate until fat solidifies. This can be prepared to this point 2 days ahead.

Spoon off fat from surface of rib braising liquid. Remove short ribs from liquid and pat dry. Strain off 1/4 cup of braising liquid. Combine the 1/4 cup braising liquid with the molasses, vinegar, hot pepper sauce and salt in a small bowl.

Have ribs at room temperature. Prepare grill (medium heat) or heat oven to 400 degrees. For grill: Place ribs on grill. Cover with grill lid or heavy duty foil. Cook until ribs are crisp and heated through, turning and basting frequently with molasses mix, about ten minutes. Serve hot.

For oven: Place ribs on foil lined flat cooking sheet. Heat ribs in oven about eight minutes, basting occasionally with the molasses mix. Finish by basting and broiling under high heat for a few minutes until ribs are crispy and heated through. Serve hot.

Richard Coyle

TROUT

Yield: 2 servings. Can be doubled.
Wine Suggestions: Riesling, Pinot Gris or Chardonnay.

Ingredients
1 medium orange
3 tbsp. chopped fresh mint
2 tbsp. olive oil
2/3 c. chopped red onion
2 tbsp. white wine vinegar
1 1/3 lb. trout, boned and cut in half lengthwise
yellow cornmeal

Directions
Grate 1 tsp. peel from the orange. Cut off remaining peel and pits and discard. Cut orange into 1/2 inch pieces. Mix these pieces with the peel and mint in a small bowl. Heat 1/2 tbsp. of oil in a skillet over medium heat.

Add onion, then vinegar and toss till just heated for 1 minute. Add onion mixture to orange and season with salt and pepper. In the same skillet (don't clean it out), sprinkle fish with water, salt pepper and cornmeal.

Heat remaining 1 1/2 tbsp. of oil over medium high heat. Add fish and sauté until crisp and just opaque in the center (about 4 minutes per side).

Transfer fish to plates and top with relish.

Elizabeth Edwards

VEAL STEW

A good one for eating today and tomorrow.

Yield: 4 servings. However, you can add more vegetables and make it last for more people.
Wine Suggestions: Merlot, Cabernet Sauvignon, Sangiovese or Zinfandel.

Ingredients
2 lbs. shoulder of veal cut into 2 inch squares
1/2 lb. fresh mushrooms
8 small spring onions, tops chopped, but not bottoms
3 stalks celery in 1 inch pieces and tops chopped

6 small carrots, cut up
3 c. beef bouillon
salt and pepper to taste
flour
butter

Directions

Flour and season the veal cubes. Sauté very gently in butter with the onion tops. Add celery and sliced mushrooms. Transfer to a deep buttered casserole. Add 3 cups of bouillon and the carrots and seasonings.

Simmer with the cover on in a medium oven of 350 degrees for 2 hours. Add more water if necessary.

Serve from the casserole.

Mrs. Cecily Littleton

VEGETABLE CASSEROLE

A simple to make vegetarian entree

Yield: 4 servings
Wine Suggestions: Riesling, Sauvignon Blanc, Pinot Grigio or Merlot.

Ingredients

2 cans Veg-All or other canned vegetable assortment
8 oz. grated sharp cheddar cheese
1 c. mayonnaise
1 medium onion, chopped
1 can of sliced water chestnuts, chopped
1 sleeve of Ritz crackers
1 stick (4 oz.) butter or margarine

Directions

Preheat oven to 350 degrees. Mix vegetables, cheese, onion, water chestnuts and mayonnaise together. Spoon mixture into a casserole dish. Crush Ritz crackers to a sand-like fine texture.

Melt a stick of butter in a pan. Remove from heat and add crushed crackers. Let crackers absorb butter, but do not fry them. Spread crackers on top of casserole, covering it completely.

Bake in the oven for 30 - 40 minutes.

Janet Saffer

VEGETARIAN PASTA

Serve with a salad for a tasty meatless meal.

Yield: 2 - 4 servings
Wine Suggestions: Sauvignon Blanc, Pinot Noir, Chardonnay or Merlot.

Ingredients
1 bunch broccoli, coarsely chopped
2 large onions, coarsely chopped
1/2 c. olive oil
1 clove of garlic, minced
ground pepper to taste
1/2 c. parmesan cheese
1 c. chick peas
8 oz. ziti or other pasta

Directions
In a large skillet, heat the olive oil. Add the onions and garlic and sauté for 10 minutes. Add broccoli and ground pepper and sauté for 10 more minutes.

Cook the pasta. When it is done, drain and return it to the pot. Toss the pasta with the skillet vegetables, parmesan cheese and chick peas.

Mary Lou Toal

Helpful Hints

Baking fish on a bed of chopped onion, celery and parsley not only makes the fish taste better, but also keeps it from sticking to the pan.

A few slices of lemon added to stewing chicken will make it more tender and tasty.

Leftover cheese can be shredded or sliced thinly and used to make tasty grilled sandwiches.

Desserts

ANGEL BAVARIAN

Truly a great party dessert.

Yield: 15 generous servings

Ingredients
2 c. milk
2 tbsp. all-purpose flour
1/8 tsp. salt
1 c. sugar
4 eggs, separated
2 envelopes unflavored gelatin
1/2 c. cold water
1/4 c. orange juice
2 tsp. grated orange rind
1- 12 oz. container of Cool Whip
1 large angle food cake broken into pieces
coconut flakes (optional)

Directions
Combine sugar, flour, egg yolks and milk in a sauce pan. Cook on stove top until mixture is slightly thickened. Add unflavored gelatin softened in 1/2 c. of cold water and grated orange rind and juice to the mixture. Stir and allow the mixture to cool.

When mixture is cool, fold egg whites (beaten until stiff), and 1 1/2 c. of thawed Cool Whip. Place small amount of custard mixture in the bottom of the pan (an angel cake pan works well), put 1/3 of the angel cake pieces in the pan and cover with the custard.

Repeat the process 2 more times until all of the cake pieces and the custard are used.

Chill in the refrigerator prior to serving. To serve, remove from pan, cover with remaining Cool Whip and sprinkle with coconut.

Mildred Burns

Helpful Hints

To make a good quick frosting, boil a small potato until soft.
Mash potato; then beat in confectioners sugar and vanilla.

APPLE DIP

Ingredients
8 oz. softened cream cheese
1 tbsp. vanilla
1/2 c. brown sugar
chopped peanuts (optional)

Directions
Mix all ingredients with electric mixer until well blended. Serve with apple slices.

Hint: dip apple slices in 7 Up or Sprite to keep from turning brown.

Barbara Ford

APPLESAUCE CAKE

An easy recipe that comes from St. George's past cookbook.

Yield: one 9 inch cake

Ingredients
1 c. applesauce
7/8 c. brown sugar
1/2 c. salad oil or melted shortening
1 3/4 c. flour
1 tsp. baking soda
1/2 tsp. salt
1 tsp. cinnamon
1/2 tsp. powdered cloves
1 tsp. ginger
1/2 c. raisins
1/2 c. nutmeats, cut in pieces

Directions
Preheat oven to 350 degrees. Butter and flour a 9 inch pan.

Mix thoroughly: applesauce, brown sugar and salad oil.

Sift together in a large bowl: flour, baking soda, salt, cinnamon, powdered cloves and ginger. Add 1/2 c. raisins and 1/2 c. nutmeats. Add the applesauce mixture and blend well. Spoon into the pan. Bake for 40 minutes at 350 degrees.

Roberta Hallowell Bowers

AUNT BETTY'S CREAM PUFFS

My aunt, Elizabeth Vassallo, was the kindest, most loving woman I have ever known. She also was a fantastic cook. I would tell her that she could put dirt in a pot and make it taste good. However, like most great Italian cooks, nothing was ever written down. She would say "about a handful" of this and "some of " that. The cream puffs were her signature dessert and unfortunately, the only recipe I recorded. Our family was blessed to have her around for 86 years.

Ingredients
1 c. water
1 c. flour
1/4 lb. butter
4 eggs
pudding, prepared as instructed on box
confectioner's sugar for dusting

Directions
Preheat oven to 375. In a saucepan combine butter and water. Bring to a boil. Add flour, stirring constantly until mixture forms a soft ball. Cook 1 minute. Remove from heat and cool 15 minutes.

Add eggs one at a time to mixture, making sure that each egg is fully incorporated before adding the next.

Drop from a well rounded tablespoon onto a lightly greased baking sheet. Cook 30 - 40 minutes until puffy and lightly brown. Cook completely.

Split each puff in half and fill with your favorite pudding. Sift confectioner's sugar on top before serving.

Donna DiPaulo

BANANA SPLIT DESSERT

Yield: Makes 10 - 14 servings

Ingredients
Crust:
2 c. graham cracker crumbs
1/4 lb. butter

Filling:
2 c. confectioner's sugar

1/2 lb. butter, softened
2 large eggs
1 tsp. vanilla
4 medium bananas
1 can (20 oz.) crushed pineapple, drained,
syrup reserved
1 1/2 c. fresh strawberries, sliced

Topping:
2 containers (9 oz.) whipped topping, thawed
1/2 to 1 c. chopped walnuts or pecans
chocolate for shaving
cherries for garnish

Directions
Crust:
Combine graham-cracker crumbs with melted butter. Press into the bottom of a 9 x 13 inch pan. Chill.
Filling:
Combine confectioner's sugar, softened butter, eggs and vanilla. Beat at high speed for 10 minutes. Spread over prepared crust. Peel bananas into pineapple syrup to prevent browning. Arrange drained bananas over filling. Spread crushed pineapple over bananas. Spread strawberries over pineapple.

Topping:
Spread whipped topping over all. Sprinkle with nuts and shaved chocolate. Garnish with cherries

Refrigerate for 8 hours before serving or freeze and let thaw one hour before serving.

Donna DiPaulo

BREAD PUDDING

The most comfortable food.

Ingredients
6 - 10 slices of stale white bread
1/2 c. raisins
6 large eggs
2 c. milk
1 c. sugar
1/4 tsp. ground nutmeg
1 tsp. vanilla
1/2 c. chopped nuts (optional)

Directions

Heat oven to 350. Lightly grease a 12 x 18 x 2 inch glass baking dish. Line baking dish with bread slices flat, side by side. Arrange several layers sprinkled with raisins. Beat eggs till foamy, whisk in the milk, sugar, nutmeg and vanilla.

Pour egg mixture over bread then press down with a spatula. Let stand for 30 minutes. Sprinkle with nuts.

Bake for 35 - 40 minutes. until custard sets. Let stand for 15 minutes. then serve with cream or whipped topping. (Also good when cool.)

Dolores Jaquith

BROWN BETTY

A childhood favorite from the previous St. George's Cookbook.

Yield: 6 servings

Ingredients

3 tbsp. butter, melted
2 c. soft bread crumbs
2 c. sliced, peeled apples
1/4 tsp. cinnamon
1/4 tsp. nutmeg
1/2 c. sugar
1/2 c. water
1 lemon rind and juice

Directions

Mix crumbs with the melted butter. Mix sugar and spices. Arrange alternate layers of crumbs and apples in a greased baking dish, beginning and ending with crumbs. Sprinkle each layer with sugar-spice mixture. Add water mixed with the lemon.

Bake covered at 350 degrees for 30 minutes. Remove cover and bake 45 minutes longer. Serve warm with hard sauce or whipped topping.

Shirley Norton

Helpful Hints

Cookies stored with a slice of bread or apple will stay moist and chewy.

BUDIN DEL CIELO (PUDDING FROM HEAVEN)

One of my favorites from Argentina.

Yield: 6 servings

Ingredients
1/2 gal. whole milk
2 1/4 lb. sugar and 2 tsp. sugar
3 whole eggs
9 egg yolks (not part of the 3 eggs above)
4 tbsp. water

Directions
Place milk and 1 1/4 lb. sugar in a pot and keep at a low boil for 1 hour and 30 minutes. The milk will turn into a brown color and it will be reduced to half the quantity. Remove from the stove and let cool slightly to a warm temperature.
In a bowl, beat the yolks and eggs. In another pot, add 2 tsps. of sugar and the water and then heat until the sugar mixed with the water gets "burnt" (dark brown color). Then coat a fluted pan with this "burnt" sugar-water mixture.

While the milk-sugar mixture is still warm, add it to the eggs and yolks mixture. Mix together and then pour into the fluted pan. Cover the fluted pan with aluminum foil and put in a "bain marie" (in a double boiler*) for 1 hour at 375 degrees.

Stick a toothpick in the pudding-if something sticks to it, keep it in the oven for a few minutes more. When it is done, let it cool down and remove it from the mold.

*Double boiler: putting the fluted pan in another larger pan/pot with boiling water (do not submerge the fluted pan but let it sit in the boiling water).

Francisco Robelo

CHEESE CAKE

Yummy dessert from St. George's past cookbook.

Yield: one 9 inch cake

Ingredients
1- 9 inch spring pan
2 lbs. cream cheese (4- 8 oz. pkgs.)

1 1/2 c. sugar
4 eggs
3/4 c. milk
1 c. sour cream (1/2 pt.)
4 tbsp. flour
1 tsp. vanilla

Directions

Beat softened cream cheese, add sugar and mix. Add eggs, one at a time, beat after each addition.

Add milk, sour cream, flour and vanilla. Mix after each addition.

Pour into a 9 inch springform pan and bake for 1 hour at 370 degrees. Cool 1/2 hour before removing from pan. Chill before serving.

Mary Bulkley

CHERRY DELIGHT DESSERT

This dessert may be made the day before and refrigerated. You can also refrigerate the cherries in the can and spread on top just before serving. A St. George's classic.

Yield: 8 - 12 servings

Ingredients
2 c. flour
2 tbsp. sugar
2 sticks margarine or butter
1- 8 oz. pkg. cream cheese
1 c. sifted powdered sugar
1 pkg. Dream Whip or 8 oz. Cool Whip, thawed
2 cans Musselman's pie cherries

Directions

Mix together flour, sugar and margarine. Spread on a cookie sheet with a fork and bake 12 minutes at 400 degrees. Cool. In a bowl, cream together cream cheese, softened to room temperature and the powdered sugar.

Prepare Dream Whip as directed on the package (or use Cool Whip) and combine with cream cheese and powdered sugar. Spread on top of cooled crust and refrigerate.

Just before serving spread pie cherries on top. Cut into squares.

Beverly McKendrick

CHOCOLATE CHIP CAKE

Yield: 1 cake

Ingredients
1 stick of butter
1 1/2 c. sugar
2 eggs
1 tsp. vanilla
2 c. flour
1 1/2 tsp. baking powder
1 tsp. baking soda
1/2 pt. of sour cream
1 tsp. cinnamon
large bag of chocolate chips

Directions
Preheat oven to 325. Grease a 13 x 9 inch pan or a tube pan (can use butter). Beat together 1 stick of butter, 1 c. sugar, eggs, vanilla.

Add in 2 c. flour, baking powder, soda and sour cream. Mix together 1/2 c. sugar and cinnamon in another small bowl.

Pour 1/2 of the batter in pan, 1/2 of the chocolate chips and 1/2 of the cinnamon mixture.

Then repeat. Bake about 25 minutes. It may take longer if using a tube pan.

Bobby Wade

CHOCOLATE REFRIGERATOR COOKIES

St. George's previous cookbook yields another great recipe.

Yield: 8 dozen cookies. Begin the day before serving.

Ingredients
1 1/4 c. soft butter or margarine
1 1/2 c. sifted confectioners sugar
1 egg
3 c. sifted cake flour
1/2 c. cocoa
1/2 tsp. salt
1 1/2 c. chopped walnuts
2 bars (4 oz. each) sweet cooking chocolate

Directions

Cream butter and sugar until light. Beat in egg. Then add the flour, cocoa and salt and mix well. Chill for several hours. Shape in 2 long rolls about 1 1 /2 inch in diameter.

Roll in nuts until coated on all sides. Wrap in waxed paper and chill overnight.

The next day, cut into 1/8 inch slices and bake in a 400 degree oven for 8 - 10 minutes. Cool. Melt chocolate over hot water and spread on the cookies.

Sara-Jean Becker

DEVIL'S FOOD SHEET CAKE

Great cake with mocha frosting.

Yield: one 13 x 9 inch cake

Ingredients

Cake:
3/4 c. soft butter or margarine
1 1/2 c. sugar
1 1/2 tsp. vanilla
2 eggs
1 3/4 c. all-purpose flour
1/2 c. unsweetened cocoa
1/4 tsp. salt
1 tsp baking soda
1/2 c. each of buttermilk and boiling water

Mocha Frosting:
1/4 c. soft butter or margarine
2 tbsp. unsweetened cocoa
3/4 tsp. instant coffee granules
1/2 tsp. vanilla
1 egg
2 c. powdered sugar

Directions

Cake:
Cream butter and sugar until blended. Add vanilla. Add eggs, one at a time, beating after each addition until light and fluffy. Stir flour, cocoa, baking soda and salt together. Add with buttermilk to creamed mixture, beating until smooth. Stir in boiling water.

Line bottom of a greased 13 x 9 in. baking pan with waxed paper. Spread batter in prepared pan. Bake at 350 degrees for 40 minutes or until pick inserted near center comes out clean. Let stand on a wire rack for 10 minutes. Turn right-side.

Turn out of pan and peel off paper. Cool thoroughly, then spread sides and top with mocha frosting.

Mocha Frosting:
In medium bowl, combine: butter, cocoa and coffee. Add egg and vanilla but do not mix. Beat in powdered sugar until smooth and of spreading consistency. If frosting is too thick to spread , add a few drops of brewed coffee or water.

Cleo Coyle

DUMP CAKE

What a great name for this cake with pineapple and fruit

Yield: 1 cake

Ingredients
1- 20 oz. large can crushed pineapple, not drained
1- 21 oz. large can pie filling, peach is best but cherry or strawberry are good too
1 pkg. yellow cake mix (without pudding) - Duncan Hines works well
3/4 c. chopped pecans
2 sticks margarine or butter

Directions
Spread undrained pineapple in a large (approx. 9 x 14 x 3) ungreased baking dish. Spread pie filling over pineapple. Sprinkle dry cake mix over all. Scatter nuts over cake mix. Slice off butter and dot over all (may use a little less than 2 sticks if it covers). Bake at 350 degrees for 1 hour. It will be juicy when removed from the oven but will thicken as it cools. Don't refrigerate. May serve with ice cream, whipped cream or alone.

Jennifer Robelo

EASY CHEESE CAKE

A treat for a busy day.

Yield: 1 cake

Ingredients
2- 8 oz. pkgs. cream cheese (softened)
3/4 c. sugar
3 eggs

Topping:
8 oz. sour cream
1/2 c. sugar
1 tsp. vanilla

Directions

Cream the cheese. Add 3/4 c. sugar and mix well. Add 3 eggs and blend with mixer until smooth. Put in a 9" pie plate. Bake 45 minutes at 325. Leave oven on while cooling for 1/2 hour. Then smooth on topping and bake for 15 minutes more. Cool, then refrigerate.

Nancy Murphy

EASY CHERRY CHOCOLATE CAKE

Yield: 1 cake

Ingredients

1 pkg. of dark chocolate cake mix (or any kind of mix you like)
1 can of cherry pie filling (or your favorite kind)
1 tsp. vanilla
2 eggs

Directions

Cake:
Beat eggs. Add cherry pie filling. Stir. Add the cake mix and vanilla. Bake in a greased 9x13 pan or Bundt pan at 350 for 45 minutes. Dust with powered sugar or frosting

Frosting:
1 c. sugar
1/3 c. milk
Bring this to a boil and add 1 bag of chocolate chips. Stir and then frost cake.

Dolores Jaquith

ELIZABETH'S SHOOFLY PIE

Yield: 2- 9 inch pies

Ingredients

2 c. boiling water
1 cup plus 3 tbsp. Grandma's molasses
2 tsp. baking soda
1/2 lb. (2 sticks butter or margarine), softened
3 c. flour
1 1/2 c. sugar
2- 9 inch unbaked pie shells

Directions

Combine boiling water, 1 c. molasses and the baking soda. Set aside while you prepare the crumbs. Combine butter or margarine, flour and sugar with your fingers to make a crumbly mixture. Brush pie shells with 3 tbsp. of the remaining molasses.

Divide the crumb mixture in half (for 2 pies). Sprinkle one half between the 2 pie shells. Pour 1/2 of the reserved molasses / soda mixture in each shell. Sprinkle with remaining crumbs, evenly.

Bake in preheated 375 degree oven for 10 minutes. Then reduce the heat to 350 degrees and continue baking another 20 minutes or until crumbs and filling are baked through.

Virginia Bracken

ENGLISH TOFFEE CANDY

Yield: about 5 pounds of candy

Ingredients

2 c. butter
2 c. sugar
1 c. ground pecans
1 lb. dark chocolate Hershey bars or dark chocolate bits
1 tsp. vanilla

Directions

Melt butter in a heavy saucepan. Add sugar, pinch of cinnamon and a few drops of water. Cook until dissolved.

Continue to cook over medium heat, stirring constantly (about 45 minutes.) until mixture becomes light caramel color and pulls away from the sides of pan or 290 degrees on a candy thermometer. The butter and sugar may separate sometimes at this point. Just pour extra butter off before pouring candy on to sheets.

Pour into ungreased cookie sheet or 2 pizza pans and cool. Melt chocolate in double boiler or microwave. When toffee is cool pour over half of chocolate and spread thin. Sprinkle with half of the nuts.

Place in refrigerator for 10 minutes to harden. Flip candy over and repeat process with the remaining chocolate and nuts. When cooled break into pieces

Ruth Legnini

FRENCH APPLE PIE

Yield: 1 pie

Ingredients
4 ripe apples
4 c. sugar
1 tsp. vanilla
1 c. milk
1 tsp. baking soda
4 c. flour

Directions
Mix dry and wet ingredients in blender. Pour into a graham cracker crust (store bought).
Bake in a preheated 400 oven for 35 - 40 minutes or until done.

Jackie Massey

GERMAN CHOCOLATE CAKE

A wonderful cake with coconut pecan frosting from our past cookbook.

Yield: 1 cake

Ingredients
Cake:
1 pkg. (4 oz.) chocolate
1/2 c. boiling water
1 c. butter
2 c. sugar
4 egg yolks
1 tsp. vanilla
2 1/4 c. sifted flour
1 tsp. baking soda
1/2 tsp. salt
1 cup buttermilk
4 egg whites, stiffly beaten

Frosting:
1 c. evaporated milk
1 c. sugar
3 egg yolks, beaten
1/2 c. butter
1 tsp. vanilla

1 1/3 c. coconut
1 c. pecans, chopped

Directions
Cake directions:
Melt chocolate in a double boiler. Cool. Cream butter and sugar until fluffy. Add yolks, one at a time. Beat well. Blend in vanilla and chocolate. Sift flour, soda and salt. Add alternately with buttermilk to chocolate mixture, beating after each addition. Fold in beaten whites. Pour into 3 - 9 inch pans, lined with a waxed paper bottom. Bake in pre-heated oven at 350 degrees for 30 - 35 minutes. Cool. Frost with coconut-pecan frosting (below)

Coconut Pecan Frosting:
Combine milk, sugar, eggs, butter and vanilla. Cook and stir over medium heat until thickened (about 12 minutes).

Add: 1 1/3 c. coconut and 1 c. pecans, chopped. Cool until thick enough to spread. Ice cake layers, top and sides.

Mary Bulkley

GRAM'S LEMON SQUARES

My mom, Evelyn Guest, is the baker in our family. She has continued the tradition passed from my German grandmother, whose buttery apple "cakes" (pies) were a lasting memory of childhood.

German treats such as springerle and pfeffernusse cookies, stollen, and apricot n' strawberry jam-layered yeast cakes were anticipated Christmas goodies that soon would fill colorful tins - ready gifts for neighbors and grandchildren.

The lemon squares are a recent addition. Mom's recipe is a good one - not too sweet and perfect when a lemony treat is needed to conclude a meal.

Ingredients
2 c. sifted flour
1/2 c. 10 x sugar
1 c. butter
4 eggs
1 2/3 c. sugar
1/3 c. lemon juice
1/4 c. flour
1/2 tsp. baking powder

Directions

Crust:

Sift together the flour and sugar. Cut the butter into the flour and sugar until the mixture clings. Press the mixture into a 13" x 9" pan. Bake at 350 degrees for 20 - 25 minutes or until lightly browned. Continue with recipe below. You will pour liquid mixture over this crust and continue baking.

Filling:

Beat together the eggs, lemon juice and 1 2/3 c. sugar. Sift together the flour and baking powder. Then stir it into the egg mixture. Pour this mixture over baked crust and return to oven for 25 minutes. While still warm sift additional 10x sugar over lemon squares. Cool and cut into bars.

Eileen McKernan

GRANDMA'S BOSTON COOKIES

This is a great make-ahead cookie recipe from the Coyle's and St. George's cooking history.

Ingredients

1 c. butter
1 1/2 c. sugar
3 eggs, well beaten
1 c. English walnuts, chopped
3 tsp. cinnamon
1 c. raisins, chopped
2 1/2 tsp. vanilla
3 c. flour
1 tsp. baking soda, dissolved in 2 tbsp. cold water

Directions

Cream butter and sugar. Add eggs, then add the rest of the ingredients in order. Mix well and put into the refrigerator overnight.

In the morning, preheat the oven to 375 degrees. Next, drop the batter off a teaspoon onto a buttered cookie sheet.

Bake the cookies for 7 - 10 minutes; watching them closely so they don't burn.

Cleo Coyle

GREAT CHOCOLATE CAKE

A great hit with our dog. She ate half a cake from the table during our book club meeting! We think you will like it too.

Yield: 16 servings

Ingredients
vegetable oil for misting the pan
flour for dusting the pan
1 pkg. plain devil's food or dark chocolate fudge cake mix (18 1/4 oz.)
1 pkg. chocolate instant pudding mix (3.9 oz.)
4 large eggs
1 c. sour cream
1/2 c. warm water
1/2 c. vegetable oil (canola, corn, safflower etc.)
1 1/2 c. semisweet chocolate chips

Directions
Place a rack in the center of the oven and preheat it to 350 degrees. Lightly mist a 12 cup Bundt pan with vegetable oil spray and then dust with flour.

Shake out the excess flour and set the pan aside.

Place the cake mix, pudding mix, eggs, sour cream, warm water and oil in a large mixing bowl. Blend with an electric mixer on a low speed for 1 minute.

Stop the machine and scrape down the sides of the bowl with a rubber spatula. Increase the speed to medium and beat 2 - 3 minutes more, scraping the sides if needed. The batter should be thick and well combined.

Fold in the chocolate chips, making sure they are well distributed throughout the batter. Pour batter into the prepared pan and place in the oven. Bake cake until it springs back when lightly pressed with your finger (45 to 50 minutes).

Remove pan from oven and cool cake on a rack for 20 minutes. Or invert onto a serving platter to serve while still warm.

Kirsten Bushick

HILDA BODENHEIMER'S BLUEBERRY PIE
A wonderful dessert straight from Lancaster County Pennsylvania

Yield: 8 servings

Ingredients
1 qt. blueberries
3/4 - 1 c. sugar
2 tbsp. flour
1 - 2 egg whites lightly beaten
nutmeg
cinnamon
juice and zest of 1 lemon
1 frozen pie crust

Directions
Mix all ingredients together. Place in defrosted pie crust. Bake in 350 - 375 degree oven for 45 - 55 minutes. Remove pie from oven and let cool. Serve with vanilla ice cream on top.

Karen Schloesser

HOMEMADE CANDY CAKES

Ingredients
4 eggs
2 c. sugar
1 c. milk
1 tsp. vanilla
2 c. flour
2 tsp. baking powder
1/2 tsp. salt
approx. 1 c. peanut butter
9 oz Hershey milk chocolate bar (or chips)

Directions
Mix eggs, sugar and milk. Add vanilla. Add dry ingredients. Mix approx. 2 minutes. Pour into a greased 11 x 17 inch deep sided, floured cookie sheet (or 2 smaller sheets). Bake at 350 for 15 - 18 minutes.

Cake will not be brown on top, test with a toothpick. While cake is hot, spread with peanut butter. When cake and peanut butter is cool, pour melted chocolate over and spread evenly. Let cool and cut into squares. It is easiest to cut when chocolate is semi-solid.

Stephanie Mahoney

HOT APPLE CAKE WITH CARAMEL RUM SAUCE

Yield: 8 - 10 servings

Ingredients

Hot Apple Cake:
1 c. (2 sticks) butter at room temperature
1 c. sugar
2 eggs, beaten
1 1/2 c. sieved all purpose flour
1 tsp. nutmeg
1 tsp. cinnamon
1 tsp. baking soda
1/2 tsp. salt
3 medium Granny Smith apples cored and finely chopped
3/4 c. chopped walnuts
1 tsp. vanilla

Caramel Rum Sauce:
1/2 c. sugar
1/2 c. firmly packed brown sugar
1/2 c. whipping cream
1/2 c. (1 stick) butter
1/4 c. rum

Directions

Hot Apple Cake:
Preheat oven to 350 degrees. Grease a 10 inch pie plate. Cream butter with sugar in a large bowl. Add eggs and beat well. Sift flour, spices, soda and salt. Blend into butter mixture. Add apples, nuts and vanilla and mix very well. Pour into prepared pie plate.

Bake until done and lightly browned, approx. 45 minutes. Serve warm with vanilla ice cream and caramel sauce.

Caramel Rum Sauce:
Combine sugars and cream in top of double boiler. Set over simmering water and cook 1 1/2 hours. Replenish water in base of double boiler as needed. Add butter and continue cooking 30 minutes. Remove from heat and beat well.

Add rum and blend thoroughly. Serve warm.

Cake and sauce can be prepared ahead and reheated before serving.

Kate Gibbons

JEWISH APPLE CAKE

Another dessert that is a blast from St. George's past.

Yield: one 10 inch cake

Ingredients
1/4 c. sugar
1 tsp. cinnamon
4 eggs
1 c. oil
1 1/2 c. sugar
1/2 c. orange juice
3 c. cubed apples (3-4 big ones)
2 1/2 tsp. vanilla
3 tsp. baking powder
3 c. flour

Directions
Mix together: sugar, cinnamon and cubed apples and set aside. Beat together: eggs, oil, sugar, orange juice, vanilla, baking powder and flour to make a batter. Stir the apple mixture into the batter. Pour into a greased 10 inch tube pan and bake at 350 degrees for 1 hour or until done.

Nancy Dorey

LEMON ANGEL MERINGUES

A special dessert recipe from St. George's past.

Yield: 4 - 6 servings

Ingredients
Lemon filling:
1 pkg. lemon pudding and pie filling
1/2 c. sugar
1 3/4 c. water
2 egg yolks
1/2 c. whipping cream
4-6 individual meringue shells

Meringue shells:
2 egg whites
1/4 tsp. cream of tartar
1/2 c. sugar

Directions

Lemon filling:

Combine pudding mix, 1/2 c. sugar and 1/4 c. of water in a saucepan. Add egg yolks and blend well. Then add the remaining 1 1/2 c. of water gradually stirring constantly. Cook and stir until mixture comes to a full boil and is thickened (about 5 minutes). Cool, stirring occasionally. Whip cream, fold into pudding and spoon into meringue shells. Chill.

Meringue shells:

Beat egg whites until foamy throughout. Add cream of tartar and beat until stiff. Add sugar, 2 tbsp. at a time, beating after each addition until sugar is blended. Then continue beating until meringue will stand in very stiff peaks.

Using a spoon, shape meringues in rounds on unglazed paper or baking sheet, make each about 3 - 4 inches diameter. Then spoon a depression in the center of each (about 1 1/2 inches deep).

Bake in slow oven (275 degrees) for 45 - 50 minutes. Cool and remove from paper. Fill meringue shells with lemon filling and serve.

Helen Lungren

LEMON BARS

Ingredients

Crust:
2 c. flour
1/2 c. powdered sugar
1 c. butter or margarine
Filling:
4 eggs
2 c. sugar
1/3 c. lemon juice
1/4 c. flour
1/2 tsp baking powder

Directions

Crust:

Sift powdered sugar and flour into a bowl. Then cut in the butter. Press into a 9 x 13 inch pan and bake at 350 degrees until it starts to brown. About 20 minutes.

Filling:

Beat the eggs and sugar until light. Add other ingredients and mix well. Pour over crust and bake in a 350 degree oven until set. About 20 - 25 minutes. Dust with powdered sugar, if desired. When it is cool, cut into 1 x 2 inch bars.

Noel Bartle

LEMON CHEESECAKE WITH GINGERSNAP CRUST

A staple for the summer!

Yield: 6 - 8 servings

Ingredients

Crust:
20 vanilla wafer cookies
10 gingersnap cookies (I use double the amount)
3 tbsp. sugar
1 tbsp. grated lemon peel
1/4 c. unsalted butter, melted (1/2 stick)

Filling:
12 oz. undiluted evaporated milk
3 1/2 oz. instant lemon pudding and pie filling mix
2 pkg. (8 oz.) cream cheese, softened
6 oz. can frozen lemonade concentrate, thawed

Top:
whipped cream

Directions

Crust:
Position rack in the center of the oven and preheat to 350 degrees. Lightly oil a 9 inch-diameter springform pan. Finely grind vanilla wafers and ginger snaps with sugar and lemon peel in a food processor. Add butter and blend well. Sprinkle crumbs over button of prepared pan; press to form bottom crust. Bake until golden brown, 12 minutes. Cool.

Filling:
In a small mixer bowl combine evaporated milk and pudding mix; beat 2 minutes. Set aside. In a large mixer bowl beat cream cheese until light. Gradually add lemonade concentrate; continue beating until smooth, light and fluffy, 3-4 minutes. Fold pudding mixture into cream cheese mixture, blending thoroughly. Pour filling into crust. Chill for 3 - 4 hours or overnight. Top with whipped cream.

Kirsten Bushick

Helpful Hints

If your baking powder isn't fresh, your baked goods my not rise.
Test it's potency by adding a bit of water to a teaspoonful. If it bubbles, it's ok.

LEMON MERINGUE PIE

This recipe I found years ago was written by a neighbor.

Yield: 1 pie

Ingredients
Custard:
1 c. water
1 c. milk
4 egg yolks
1 1/2 c. sugar
1/4 tsp. salt
4 tbsp. cornstarch
juice of 3 lemons
grated rind of 2 lemons
1 tsp. butter

Meringue:
4 egg whites
8 tbsp. sugar

1 pie crust

Directions
Custard:
Mix together the water and milk. Beat in 4 egg yolks. Then in another bowl combine the dry ingredients: sugar, salt and cornstarch.

Now combine the dry ingredients with the milk mixture.

Next add the lemon juice, lemon rind and the butter. Cook in the top of a double boiler over hot water until very thick. Stir almost constantly for 25 minutes of actual cooking time.

Meringue:
Beat egg whites until very stiff. Slowly beat in sugar. Put custard in your favorite cooked pie crust and cover to the sides with meringue.

Bake in moderate oven (350 degrees) until delicately browned.

Miriam McFarland

LINZERTORTE

From Austria. A rich dessert. Pastry dough may be made earlier, frozen if well wrapped.

Yield: 10 small servings

Ingredients
2 c. flour
1/8 tsp. ground cloves
1/4 tsp. cinnamon
1 1/3 c. finely chopped ground almonds
1/2 c. plus 1 1/2 oz. white sugar
2 tsp. grated lemon peel
2 mashed hard cooked egg yolks
1 1/3 c. soft butter or margarine
2 raw egg yolks beaten with 1 tsp. vanilla
1 1/2 c. thick raspberry jam
2 tbsp. light cream or milk for brushing pastry

Directions
Mix flour, cloves, cinnamon, almonds, sugar, lemon peel and hard cooked egg yolks. Then beat in the butter, raw yolks and vanilla.

Form a flat circle of dough and chill in refrigerator. When cold enough to shape, using your hands spread 1/4 in. thick in a 10 1/2 inch springform pan.

Extend dough 1/2 in. up the sides of the pan. Spread base with jam-evenly distributed. Place 1/2 in. wide strip of dough in an X pattern over jam. Run a sharp knife around the edge of sides of pan.

Fold extended edge of dough over ends of dough strips, to make a border approximately 1/4 in. wide. Brush exposed pastry with cream or milk.

Refrigerate for 1/2 hour. Heat oven to 350. Bake on middle shelf for 40 - 50 minutes. Cool to room temperature. Sprinkle with confectioners sugar. Serve with whipped cream (optional)

Kate Gibbons

Helpful Hints

For extra moist and chewy brownies, add 1/3 bag of miniature marshmallows to the batter.

MOTHER'S DAY NEW YORK CHEESE CAKE

Copied from mother's handwritten recipe. Best ever!

Yield: 1 cake

Ingredients
2- 8oz. pkg of cream cheese
1 lb. cottage cheese
1 1/2 c. sugar
4 eggs
3 tbsp. cornstarch
3 tbsp. flour
1 1/2 tsp. lemon juice
1 tsp. of grated rind
1 tsp. vanilla
1/2 c. melted butter
1 pt. sour cream

Directions
Preheat oven to 325. Grease 9 inch springform pan. There is no crust. Beat cream cheese and cottage cheese. Add sugar, eggs, cornstarch, flour, lemon juice and rind. Add melted butter and sour cream.

Bake 1 hour and 10 minutes. Turn off heat and leave cool in oven for 2 hours. Cool for 3 hours and refrigerate for 8 hours, or 24 hours if you can. Remove sides of pan and serve from bottom of pan. Top with fruit pie filling or serve on the side.

Dolores Jaquith

MRS. ANDERSON'S CHOCOLATE MOUSSE

Yield: 4 servings

Ingredients
1 bag semisweet chocolate bits (6 oz.)
3/4 cup milk, scalded
1 egg
2 tbsp. sugar
1 tsp. vanilla
dash of salt

Directions

Place all ingredients, except the milk, into a blender. Gradually add the milk. Blend for 1 minute until smooth. Pour into cups and refrigerate until the mousse sets, approximately 2 - 3 hours.

Top with Crème de Menthe, pecans or whipped cream.

Karen Schloesser

PHYLLIS' RICE PUDDING

A creamy rice pudding cooked on top of the stove.

Yield: 6 servings

Ingredients

1/2 gal. milk (whole milk is best)
1 c. water
2 tbsp. butter
1 c. rice (not "minute rice")
1/4 c. sugar
3 eggs
1 tbsp. vanilla
1 c. sugar

Directions

Combine first five ingredients in large pan and bring to a boil very slowly (important).

Reduce heat and let bubble for 28 minutes with lid askew, stirring occasionally. Meanwhile, in bowl beat eggs, vanilla, and sugar.

When milk/rice mixture is ready, turn off heat and slowly pour egg mixture into milk in a small stream, stirring constantly. It will thicken as you add the egg mixture.

Add any spices or seasoning you like - a little pumpkin pie spice and a little grated lemon rind is nice. Pour into bowl and sprinkle with cinnamon. Enjoy!

Eileen Kammerer

Helpful Hints

Heat fruits and raisins in the oven to make plumper before adding to cake and pudding batter.

PUMPKIN PIE

A wonderful recipe from the previous St. George's Cookbook.

Yield: 2 pies

Ingredients
1 large can pumpkin
1 c. dark brown sugar
1 c. sugar
4 eggs
2 tsp. salt
1 1/2 tsp. ginger
3 tsp. cinnamon
1 tsp. allspice
4 c. rich milk (1 can evaporated milk added to whole milk to equal 4 cups)
2 unbaked pie crusts

Directions
Mix together all ingredients except milk. Gradually add milk keeping mixture smooth. Pour into unbaked pie crusts. Bake in a 425 degree oven for 15 minutes. Then lower the heat to 350 degrees and bake for 35 more minutes or until firm.

Cora Kinsley

RICOTTA CHEESE COOKIES

These are delicious any time. Around the holidays, you can add food coloring to the icing to be festive.

Ingredients
Cookies:
1 lb. ricotta cheese
3 eggs
2 c. sugar
2 tsp. vanilla
1/2 lb. butter
4 c. flour
1 tsp. baking soda

Icing:
1 box 10X sugar
4 tbsp. butter, melted
2 tsp. vanilla
a little bit of milk

Directions

Preheat oven to 375. In large bowl mix ricotta cheese, eggs, sugar, vanilla and butter. In a small bowl mix flour and baking soda. Mix dry ingredients gradually into the cheese mixture. Drop by spoonfuls onto an ungreased cookie sheet (it will be like a thick cake batter). Bake for 12 - 14 minutes. Cool.

Mix the ingredients for the icing. Spread on the icing. Store, with wax paper between layers in a cool place.

Maria Soda

SIX MINUTE CHOCOLATE CAKE

A long time favorite of the Duffey's. Quick easy and very tasty!

Yield: 1 cake.

Ingredients
1 c. sugar
1 1/2 c. flour
1/3 c. cocoa
1 tsp. baking soda
1/2 tsp. salt
2 tsp. vanilla
1/2 c. oil
1 c. cold water
2 tbsp. white vinegar
powdered sugar to sprinkle over top

Directions

In a square 8 inch or a round 9 inch cake pan measure all ingredients - except for the vinegar. Stir them well with a wire whisk (or fork) until they are thoroughly blended. Add the vinegar and stir quickly to thoroughly blend in and immediately place in a pre-heated 375 oven.

There must be no delay after the vinegar is added. Bake for 20 - 25 minutes (usually takes longer) or until the center is slightly puffed and the sides begin to pull away. Cool.

Makes one layer cake. Sprinkle with the powdered sugar or frost with chocolate icing. We like to lay a paper doily on the cool cake and sprinkle the sugar through the holes just before serving.

Betty Duffey

TANDY CAKE

Yield: 1 cake

Ingredients

4 eggs
1 tsp. vanilla
pinch of salt
1 tsp. baking powder
2 c. flour
2 c. sugar
2 tbsp. oil
1 c. milk
peanut butter
1- 12 oz. or 14 oz. chocolate bar

Directions

Beat eggs till lemon colored. Add vanilla and mix. Sift salt, flour, sugar and baking powder into a bowl. Add sifted ingredients, oil and milk to eggs and mix.

Bake on a greased 11 x 17 x 3/4 inch cookie sheet for 15 minutes at 350 degrees. Take from the oven and spread with peanut butter. When cool, melt a 12 oz. or 14 oz. chocolate bar and pour over the top. Refrigerate to harden the chocolate.

Sara-Jean Becker

UNIQUE BAVARIAN CREAM WITH FRUIT SAUCE

Easy but looks "gourmet". Sauce can be made the day before.

Yield: 6 - 8 servings

Ingredients

1 envelope unflavored gelatin
1/4 c. cold water
1 8 oz. pkg of cream cheese (regular or light)
4 1/2 c. white sugar
1 tsp. vanilla
dash of salt
1 c. milk
1 c. double cream, whipped
fruit sauce (apricot or raspberry)

Directions

Soften gelatin in cold water. Stir over low heat until dissolved. Combine softened cream cheese, sugar, vanilla and salt, mixing until well blended. Slowly mix in milk and gelatin. Chill until slightly thickened.

Fold in whipped cream. Pour into lightly oiled 1 qt. mold. Chill until firm. Unmold, decorate with a little sauce, pass around remainder of sauce.

Fruit Sauce:
Quick version: 1- 10 oz. jar of good apricot preserve combined with 1/3 c. dry white wine. Mix well. chill until serving time.
or
Soak 3/4 lb. dried apricots overnight in water to just cover. Drain, replace water just to cover. If you do not have a blender-chop apricots into small pieces. Add 2 tbsp. light brown sugar. Place in a small saucepan bring to a boil, lower heat and simmer covered until apricots are soft. Cool to luke warm. Puree in a blender and cool.
or
2 pkgs. frozen raspberries in juice, sweeten to taste. Defrost. Strain to remove seeds.
or
Serve with any fresh fruit. Any sweet liqueur 1 - 2 tbsp. may be added to sauces

Kate Gibbons

Wine &
Beverages

SUMMER SANGRIA

On a warm summer evening this is a great treat to serve your guests

Yield: 1 happy party group.

Ingredients
2 liters of red Burgundy table wine
2 oranges, sliced thin
2 lemons, sliced
a sprinkle of cinnamon
2 - 4 oz. cognac
1/3 c. sugar
half a bottle (1/2 qt.) of club soda

Directions
In a large bowl, pour the wine and add the sliced oranges, sliced lemon, cinnamon and the cognac. Mix everything with a wooden spoon. Then add the sugar (depending on your taste, add a little bit more if needed, but overall it shouldn't be more than 1/2 c.).

Just before serving, add the club soda and ice. You can also add Triple Sec and more oranges for more "power".

Francisco Robelo

FISH HOUSE PUNCH

A hearty libation to create and have at a party.

Yield: 6 servings

Ingredients
4 oz. lemon juice
3/4 lb. fine granulated sugar, dissolved in a little water
8 oz. brandy
4 oz. peach liqueur
8 oz. Jamaican rum
2 tbsp.. Angostura Bitters
2 pints or more carbonated water

Directions
Pour ingredients into a punch bowl in the order listed. Ice and serve. For individual Fish House Punch use the same ingredients, in proportionate quantities.

RUM PARTY PUNCH

A good punch for a large party.

Yield: 20 servings

Ingredients
1 qt. fresh strawberries
6 oz. sugar
1 qt. dark Jamaica rum or New England rum
3 oranges, juiced
1 pint cold tea
1 pint brandy
1 qt. champagne
pineapple slices, diced apple or orange slices to float on the top of the punch.
maraschino cherries for garnish

Directions
Place the strawberries and sugar in the dark rum and allow to soak for 2 hours. Put 1 large piece of ice in the center of a punch bowl and pour the mixture on the ice. Add the juice of 3 oranges, the cold tea, brandy and champagne. Stir slowly, adding fresh fruit, sliced pineapple, diced apples or slices of orange and maraschino cherries.

Karen Schloesser

ROSY GLOW PUNCH

A nonalcoholic punch for a large party.

Yield: 50 1/2 cup servings

Ingredients
3 quarts cranberry juice cocktail
1- 12 oz. can lemonade concentrate, thawed
1/2 gallon raspberry sherbet
1 quart ginger ale

Directions
Combine cranberry juice cocktail and lemonade. Stir well. Chill. Just before serving pour in to a 4 quart punch bowl. Add scoops of sherbet. Slowly add ginger ale.

A St. George's Tradition

WASSAIL BOWL

A past tradition at St. George's.

Yield: enough for a large party. Make the day before.

Ingredients
2 lemons, sliced
2 oranges, sliced
2 c. sugar
1 jar whole allspice
1/2 jar whole cloves
6 pieces cinnamon
2 tsp. ginger
5 c. orange jiuce
2 c. lemon juice
2 gal. Burgandy wine

Directions
Mix everything except the wine and juices. Bring to a boil. Reduce heat and barely simmer uncovered for 1/2 hour to 45 minutes. Strain. Mix with wine and juices. Let sit overnight.

RUM PUNCH

This is our traditional Christmas dinner punch which we make only for that special occasion.

Serves a crowd

Ingredients
1 qt. orange juice
1 qt. pineapple juice (unsweetened)
6 oz. lime juice
1 qt. club soda
1 qt. dark rum

Directions
Pour above ingredients into a punch bowl over a block of ice or ice cubes.

For a single drink: In a highball glass over ice cubes pour 1 1/2 oz. each of rum, orange juice and pineapple juice and 1/4 oz. lime juice. Fill glass with club soda. Stir. Garnish with a stick of pineapple

Mary Lou Toal

LIMONCELLO

On a rainy night in Milan, after Donna and I had a wonderful Italian meal, 2 limon-cellos miraculously appeared at the table. We were hooked. Since then we have had the pleasure of introducing this refreshing, unique libation to our guests. The process takes several days but is well worth the effort. Several of our guests have remarked that the store-bought brand cannot compare with this homemade recipe.

Ingredients
3 large, thick skinned lemons
2 c. unflavored 80-proof vodka
1 1/2 c. water
1 c. sugar

Directions
Soak the lemons in cold water for 2 hours. Dry well.

Using a vegetable peeler or zester, remove only the yellow outer peel, leaving the bitter white part on the lemons. Pour the vodka into a clean wide-mouthed jar. Add the lemon peel and stir.

Replace the lid and store in a dark room at room temperature for 72 hours. Place the peeled lemons in a plastic bag and refrigerate. Combine the water and sugar in a saucepan. Bring to a boil over medium-high heat, stirring to dissolve the sugar.

Remove from heat. Juice the reserved lemons and stir 1/4 c. of the lemon juice into the water-sugar mixture. Save the remaining juice for another use. Discard the lemons.

Let the juice-water mixture cool about 2 hours, and then add to the jar with the vodka and lemon peel.

Close jar and return to the dark place for another 36 hours.

Strain vodka-lemon mixture into clean bottles or jars with caps or lids. Freeze.

Limoncello is best served straight from the freezer, poured into tiny glasses at the end of the meal.

Don Di Paulo

PERFECT BOURBON MANHATTAN

Ingredients
3 oz. Makers' Mark Boubon
1/2 oz. sweet vermouth
1/4 oz. dry vermouth
3 dashes D'Angastora bitters

Directions
Pour 3 oz. Makers' mark Bourbon, 1/2 oz. sweet vermouth, 1/4 oz. dry vermouth and 3 dashes of Angostura bitters over ice cubes into a glass mixer. (Commonly referred to as a pint glass). Stir for about 30 revolutions and strain over a cherry into a chilled martini glass.

Call a cab.

Pete Ricci

Selecting and Enjoying Wine
The St. George's Method

The Big Question

OK. You have found a tantalizing recipe for dinner this evening. You have even talked to the author of the recipe - they sit in the pew in back of you each Sunday. The dinner will be terrific - your guests will talk about it all the way home. One question remains, and it is a horrible one - What wine will you serve??

It isn't an unimportant question. Good wine can add immeasurably to a dinner's enjoyment. In my home, since I know more about good wine than good cooking, it routinely masks flaws in the dinner itself.

On the other hand, a poor wine, or the decidedly wrong wine, can be an ongoing distraction to an otherwise wonderful dinner.

The Dilemma

Wine is a complex and complicated subject. If you feel overwhelmed by it, you are on the right track. There are thousands of wineries, dozens of grape varieties, scores of vintages available and that is even before you get to the matter of soil, viticulture (grape farming) and winemaking technique itself.

For those who find the subject interesting, there is a lifetime's supply of literature and wine courses available.

For those who enjoy the taste and the variety, you could try 50 different wines a day and never try the same wine twice - in your lifetime.

So, it is great for those folks. But what if you just want to select a good quality, reasonably priced bottle of wine to enhance that dinner?

The Solution

This chapter is dedicated to helping the relative wine novice select and enjoy a good bottle of reasonably priced ($8 - $20) wine with any of the recipes in this, or any other cookbook.

There are a few caveats:

We are going to do some heavy editing of the wine literature to get this to a few guidelines, so this is a starting point; it is not all inclusive.

There is truth to the maxim that for every rule, there is an exception.

There is a relationship between price and quality in this price range. When one selects a really expensive wine (over $30) - as the price increases the issue may be less quality than availability (some wineries make only a few hundred bottles of certain wines) or snob-appeal. But in our price range, on average, a well selected $20 bottle will be better than an $8 bottle.

Matching Wine with Food

Wine is food. This may be the most important statement you will ever learn about wine. It is a farm product, a fruit (generally a grape variety) which is specially handled and treated to create an alcoholic (8 - 15% alcohol for table wines) beverage.

Wine matches food when it complements it. This is easier to taste than describe - you probably know when this has happened - when you take a sip of wine, note that you enjoy it and it takes you back to the dinner. The wine match isn't working if you feel the need to take a drink of water before returning to your food.

Wine color has nothing to do with whether it matches the food. That said, the adage of red wine with meat and white with fish does tend to work because of the qualities inherent in many red and white wines.

The real trick is matching up the wine's body, acidity, tannin and sweetness with the food. The wine's flavors, such as whether it is "redolent of huckleberries and licorice," is the stuff of would be wine connoisseurs with little else going on in their lives, is highly subjective and is mostly irrelevant to the rest of us.

Here is what you should know about body, acidity, tannin and sweetness:

Body - is how "heavy" the wine feels in your mouth. Higher alcoholic content (the percentage is on the label) equates to more body. Both red and white wines can be full or light bodied.

Richer, heavier, sauce laden foods tend to go best with fuller bodied wines. Lighter dinners and many appetizers match up best with lighter bodied wines. Makes sense, right?

Acidity - is primarily a white wine issue - this is the matter of how tart the wine is. Think of biting into a green apple - that is high acidity. When there is little acidity, the wine is called flabby. More acidity helps a wine stand up to a complex dish.

Tannin - is found only in red wines (it is from the red grape skins) and is what makes your mouth pucker on the sides - it tends to dry out your mouth. High tannin goes best with fattier foods. A high tannin wine can enhance a lamb or duck dish, for example, because it actually cuts through the fattiness of the food in your mouth.

Tannins soften with age. So, the older the wine, on average, the more mellow the tannic wine will become. Young tannic wines are very drying in the mouth, a quality which some can find unpleasant.

Sweetness - is from the sugar in the grape. When all the grape sugar present in the grape is fermented into alcohol - the wine is considered dry. If some of the sugar goes unfermented, some sweetness remains in the wine. Most table wines are relatively dry; truly sweet wines such as port and sauternes are reserved for dessert. That said, a touch of sweetness, like one might find in a German Riesling white wine, can complement a dinner which has a touch of sweetness in it - for example a chutney based sauce.

Wine Choices - According to the Grape

There are many. This is where the heavy editing comes in.

Each wine grape has its own distinctive characteristics - though that is modified by the area the grape is grown in, the soil, the winemaker's style and other factors. Given our minimalist approach to wine selection, we are going to concentrate on the great wine grapes of the world - red and white.

Red Wine Grapes

Cabernet Sauvignon

Where Produced - Perhaps the most ubiquitous red wine grape - grown in California, France (referred to as Medoc or Bordeaux or Claret), Italy, Australia and elsewhere.

Style - Generally deep red, full bodied, with much tannin and dry - very intense and aromatic wines.

Food Matches - Best with hearty meals, like beef, lamb, Northern Italian dishes, duck and the like.

Age - Need some "bottle age" to mellow out the tannin - a minimum of two years, 3 - 5 is much better. They are very long lasting; when treated appropriately, good vintages can easily improve for 20 years and more.

Price - A fairly expensive grape and wine to produce. It needs to age more than other varieties, so it is difficult to find good ones for less than $10/bottle. A higher priced, well selected wine will reward the purchaser.

Special note: California cabernets are, on average, "bigger" wines and are often more appealing to beginners than their French counterparts, which tend to be more complex and refined. Italian and Australian cabernets increasingly are of a California model.

Merlot

Where Produced - California, Washington State, France (called Pomerol or St. Emilion), South America and many, many other places.

Style - "Softer" and easier to appreciate than Cabernet. Almost purple, moderate tannin, dry wine. Some refer to it as lush.

Food Matches - A fairly safe wine with all but white fish and spicy dishes. Merlot's softness and moderate tannins make it a reasonable match with beef dishes, excellent with chicken and veal. Can get lost with strong flavored dinners.

Age - Unlike Cabernet need minimal bottle age to be pleasant. Two years will do for most. They develop well with more age.

Price - Fine Merlots are among the most expensive wines in the world, but it is an inexpensive and plentifully planted grape, so there are good values beginning at $8/bottle.

Pinot Noir

Where Produced - France (Burgundy & Champagne), Oregon and cooler parts of California (Carneros).

Style - Much more subtle than other red wines, some would say takes more tasting experience to enjoy. Medium red color, medium body, light tannin, dry red wine.

Food matches - Wonderful with those complex dinners with more sophisticated flavors - lots of sauces and accompaniments. Wasted on steak where it will be overpowered, terrific with lighter game, veal, salmon and perhaps tuna, non-tomato sauce pastas.

Age - Good in its youth. 1 - 2 years is fine.

Price - There is no bargain Pinot Noir. It will tend to hug the upper end of our price range - inexpensive Pinot Noirs start at about $15.

Sangiovese

Where Produced - Italy (Chianti is a blended wine made primarily from Sangiovese), California.

Style - Wide range, from deep ruby, medium body, big tannins (Riservas from Chianti) to lighter wines. Closer to a Pinot Noir than a Cabernet Sauvignon.

Food matches - Just what you would think of a wine from Italy. Very accommodating except with shellfish and white fish.

Age - Good in its youth, but also ages well.

Price - Can be very good value - even the lower priced ones tend to be interesting.

Zinfandel

Where Produced - California - the quintessential American wine.

Style - Most are deep red, full bodied, moderate to heavy tannin, very dry wines.

Food Matches - Best with "bigger" foods - good barbeque wine. Best red Thanksgiving wine.

Age - Good when young, best of the reds here. But ages well up to 5 - 7 years.

Price - Has become trendy and price has followed. Expect to pay $10 - $15.

Special Note: White Zinfandel (blush) wine is a poor imitation of the red zinfandel described above. It is a "beginner's wine" and is not particularly useful to serve with most dinners.

Syrah

Where Produced - France (Rhone, Chateuneuf du Pape), California, Australia (Shiraz), South Africa, elsewhere.

Style - Deep red, medium to full bodied, lots of tannin and dry.

Food Matches - Similar to Cabernet.

Age - Needs 2 - 3 years to gain balance.

Price - Wide range, but generally a good value. Plenty of good Rhones and Australian Shiraz at $8 - $12.

White Wine Grapes

Chardonnay

Where Produced - France (Burgundy, Chablis and Champagne), California, Italy, Australia, South America, and virtually everywhere else.

Style - Full bodied, yellow-white acidic wine, rather dry - has become synonymous with white wine. California versions tend to be aged in wood and have an "oaky" flavor that many find desirable.

Food Matches - Hard to go wrong with anything light or white, including chicken and lighter pork dishes. Lost on red meat and with red sauces.

Age - Unless you really know your wines, go with younger chardonnays 1 - 2 years old.

Price - Little under $10 is worth drinking, though there is plenty of product. Better wines are $12 - $20 a bottle.

Sauvignon Blanc

Where Produced - California, France (Sancerre, Loire, Pouilly-Fume, Sauternes), South America, elsewhere.

Style - Very light, almost water color wine, light body, fruity, dry (except for Sauternes where the winemaking technique creates a sweet wine), tart.

Food Matches - In general, a much better aperitif than Chardonnay, good with shellfish and lighter fishes; goat cheese is a perfect match. Cannot stand up to more substantial meat dishes, although acidity makes for an interesting match with red sauces.

Age - The fresher the better. French versions age better than domestic.

Price - Inexpensive. Hard to understand why would spend any more than $15 for domestic versions, and many good ones are available for $8 - $12.

Pinot Gris

Where Produced - In Italy, this is Pinot Grigio; it is also produced in Germany, Alsace and Oregon.

Style - Varies somewhat. Italian versions are fairly simple- pleasant, fruity wines, light bodied - something like a Sauvignon Blanc but less complex. Those from Oregon, and to some extent Germany and Alsace, have more body and depth. Generally dry and light acidity.

Food Matches - Depends again on origin - Italian wines are best as an aperitif or with very light dishes. Oregon pinot gris has more body and is wonderful with salmon and shellfish.

Age - Generally the fresher the better - no more than 2 - 3 years unless you know what you are doing.

Price - Relatively inexpensive, $8 - $12, although the more expensive Pinot Grigios and Pinot Gris can be exceptional wines.

Riesling

Where Produced - Germany, Alsace, New York State, Washington State, New Zealand.

Style - Mostly light bodied, good acidity, floral and fruity wines. Dry to off dry. Low alcohol due to short growing season for grapes.

Food Matches - Perhaps the best white wine to match with food. So substantial that can match up with all but the most beefy dishes.

Age - Good in its youth. 1 - 2 years, but ages well too.

Price - Expect to pay $12 - $20 for good Riesling. Inexpensive domestic versions are rarely good quality

Special Note: Riesling is the quintessential German wine. At one time, it was among the most

sought after and expensive wines in the world. Then Blue Nun and Liebfraumilch appeared, the German wine market became associated with these insipid, overly sweet wines, and it crashed. Consequently, the best white wine values in the world today can be found in German Rieslings. Look for the words Qualitswein mit Pradikat on the label to get good quality. In German - trocken means dry. Halbtrocken means off dry (slightly sweet).

Other Wines you may have heard of:

Champagne - This is actually a place, in France. It has become synonymous with sparkling wine, although sparkling wine is produced in Germany, Spain, the U.S. and elsewhere with fine results. Sparkling wines range from extremely dry (Brut) to sweet (Sec). They are made from both red and white grapes (Chardonnay, Pinot Noir and Riesling primarily). While associated primarily with celebratory events, good sparkling wines are an excellent accompaniment to food in the same way that their non-sparkling grape counterparts would be.

Beaujolais - This is a location in France that makes a fruity wine from the Gamay grape. It is drunk very young, often within months of bottling. It is seen by some as a good accompaniment to turkey, but is generally considered too grapey to complement most fine dinners.

Rose - Rose wines are made from red grapes. The wine skins are left to ferment for a short period of time and they impart a pink color to the wines. There are some very fine rose wines, particularly from France, which are terrific summer wines. But the market for fine rose wines is compromised by blush wines from California, some of which are made from the zinfandel grape, but others are low quality white grape wines with coloring added.

Port - This sweet wine, the best wine in the world to accompany most cheeses, is made in Portugal. Vintage ports are very expensive - beyond the range of this guide. There are good value tawny ports in the $12 - $20 range.

Buying and Storing Wine

The Purchase

If you are a relative newcomer to wine, and you walk into a wine store without a plan, looking for a "good bottle of wine", you will likely find it a frustrating experience. You need a plan, not a big plan, but a plan. Before you go to the store, know the following:

What wines will reasonably match the food you are serving?

Each dinner recipe in this cookbook offers a suggestion. Or quickly review the grape descriptions noted previously and identify the grapes, and consequently the wines, which are of interest to you. Note which countries produce that wine.

How much do you want to spend?

This is up to you, within the constraints of the marketplace cost for certain wines. But decide it in advance, maybe subject to a few dollars either way.

Where will you shop?

In Pennsylvania you will be heading off to a state run wine store, which is generally too bad. If you live in New Jersey or Delaware or other progressive states (at least as far as wine goes) you will have much more selection. But even in a "state store" you can find good wine - it is just that you will be paying too much for it.

Let's say that you are serving salmon with a light sauce. You know from the previous section that certain wines are a great match with salmon, or you just look at the recipe (if it is in this cookbook) and note the following recommendations:

Pinot Gris, Pinot Noir, Chardonnay, Riesling

Assume that you want to spend about $12. Well, you can pretty much rule out the Pinot Noir, as noted in the previous section, because they are quite expensive, and even if you find one at $12 it will likely be dubious.

Most wine stores are organized by country and, within that, by grape. So quickly check the grape list to see which country each grape is produced within. You quickly find:

Pinot Gris - Oregon is best when serving with a dinner like this.

Chardonnay - Produced almost everywhere and it is called chardonnay everywhere except in France where it is Burgundy, Chablis and Champagne.

Riesling - Germany and Alsace.

You will have many, many alternative wines to choose from - which can be fun but frustrating at the same time. It may be that you want to consider your preferences before you even get in the car. You have probably had a lot of Chardonnay already - maybe Pinot Gris or Riesling will be more interesting for you. Or if it is to be a Chardonnay, maybe a French version instead of the Kendall-Jackson (California) you usually buy.

You may also want to keep in mind the wines which are produced in the area in which your dinner is created. It is simply true that Northern Italian wines tend to go better with Northern Italian recipes, etc. It isn't that surprising that Pinot Gris from Oregon complements salmon from the Pacific Northwest.

When you get to the store, plan on spending a little time perusing the stock - you will learn a lot and it will make your next visit more productive. Learn how they have organized their wines. Beyond the country of origin organization, you will generally find there are three basic wine sections:

1.   The fine wine area - bottles under locked glass selling for what used to be considered a good week's paycheck.

2.   Inexpensive wines, lined up on grocery shelves like vodka and bourbon, with names which you have probably seen in full page magazine spreads.

3.   Good, moderate priced wines, lying on their sides, usually with stock underneath the display bottle.

You have probably guessed that you are going to section 3.

If you would like to splurge on section 1 - that is terrific but is beyond what we are covering here. My advice is stay away from section 2. While section 2 may hold a few decent wines for everyday quaffing, they are rarely good product. They are industrially produced wines, not the farm products we are looking for. The companies that produce them spend more on advertising than they do on quality fruit and winemaking.

Avoid wines that are standing upright on a shelf and sell in 1.5 liter bottles, in the same way you would avoid wines that come in gallon jugs or cardboard boxes.

The wines you are looking to buy are produced by vintners producing a few thousand bottles per year. The bottles in section 2 are being produced by the hundreds of thousands annually.

The wines you wish to purchase may be aged in oak barrels for a period of time. The wines in section 2 are frequently pumped over wood chips to give a sense of oak flavor.

Back to your salmon dinner. When you go to Section 3, in the Oregon section, you will see the store's selection of Pinot Gris. Check out the prices and see if there is a match at all. While you are there you will see the Oregon Pinot Noir - note what they have even though it is out of your price range on this one.

When you go to Alsace and Germany looking for that Riesling, you will quickly find that your price range will narrow you down to a few sections. If German, look for the Qualitswein mit Pradikat language, and perhaps trocken (dry). If you feel that you don't have enough choice, open up to the Chardonnays, which will take you to California

And now you have a problem, because even in the most ordinary state store, you probably now have a choice of 10 - 15 wines to make. Some suggestions:

Decide if you are being adventurous (i.e. Pinot Gris) or not (i.e. California Chardonnay).

If the store appears serious about selling wine, there may be someone who is willing to offer advice - just don't get bound by their thoughts.

Look for wine ratings - a variety of wine magazines rate wines on a 100 point scale and wine stores tend to publish them next to the wines. You will never see anything rated under 80. Anything over 85 is considered good by these publications. You can trust the Wine Advocate (WA). The Wine Spectator (WS) is more frequently seen but is, in my experience, less reliable. There are other rating groups - when in doubt these are all useful pieces of information.

If you are looking at a red wine where bottle age improves the wine - consider the older wine.

Keep in mind that California and French wines tend to be more expensive on average - so the quality/price ratio may be less than something you are looking at from another area.

Avoid wines with names that sound like subdivisions in Chester County and sell in the $8 - $10 range. You know the type - I will make a few up here - Oak Bridge; Raven's Nest, River Valley. They are, generally speaking, Section 2 wines which are being marketed upscale for Section 3. With more expensive wines this rule does not apply.

When in doubt, avoid wines with gaudy or even overly designed labels and certainly those with chic bottles. Keep in mind - wine is a farm product. The best values in wine in the world are those produced in small amounts by people who care about the fruit. On average they do not invest in label design. They tend to sell wine with labels which are simple in appearance and often carry their family name.

Storage

Heat and low humidity are the enemies of wine (farm product - remember). Assuming you have not created a below ground level wine cellar, the best place to store wine is your refrigerator. It is as simple as that. When you start collecting so much wine that this is no longer practical, buy a book on storing wine.

Serving Wine

There isn't much to know about serving wine, but attention to a few key issues is important or your investment may very well be wasted. But it is easy.

Temperature

Red wines should be served at room temperature, as the old adage suggests. But that old adage was created in England, before central heating was created. So, the right temperature is in the high 50's, low 60's. I don't know anyone who uses a thermometer for this kind of thing, but you certainly want to take the wine out of the refrigerator an hour or so before serving.

If it is still too cold when you open it - don't worry, it will warm up. You can tell if it is too cold - it won't have much taste.

White wines should be colder - the low 50's are good. But this is warmer than most refrigerators, so you still should take the wine out beforehand.

Remove the cork

If you don't have one, get a corkscrew where the screw part looks something like a roll of barbed wire, instead of a wood screw. Sooner or later the latter type will just drill a hole in your cork as opposed to removing it. Throw out the cork - the time honored sniffing of the cork is an affectation - it makes no sense.

Use the right glasses

Forget all that stuff about which glasses go with which wines. Buy a set of large glasses (12 oz. or more), that curve inward at the top (to funnel the aroma), are clear (no cut glass or colors), and moderately thin (not like your day to day water glasses). Good wine glasses sell for $4 - $6 at Ikea, Pottery Barn and the like. Or you can spend $75 for Riedel crystal.

Pour

Just pour. Pour heartily and then twist your wrist so the last drops of red wine don't land on your white tablecloth. If you pour too slowly the wine will be all over your white tablecloth.

Enjoy the Evolution

Good wine evolves in the glass, over time. It changes, mostly improves and evolves. Note the changes which occur and enjoy them.

Keith Pryor

Those Earlier Cookbooks

They were mentioned amongst the recipes, and here are images of this book's predecessors

Patrons Page

Publication of this book was made possible by the generosity of the following people

Bob and Cheryl Ames
Lance, Allison, Peyton and Piper Billingsley
Heather S. Bonner
Mrs. Mildred H. Burns
The Bushick Family
Brian and April Chester
Cleo Coyle
Claire and Richard Coyle
The DeBlois - Bob, Linda, Ryan and Patti
Don and Donna DiPaulo
Father Bill and Betty Duffey
Michael Fox
The Garritys
Ian and Kate Gibbons
Sally Hale
Joe and Liz Havens
Dick and Dolores Jaquith
June and Jeff Jaquith
Paul Joslin and Catherine Mallam-Joslin
Paul and Eileen Kammerer
Cathy and Frank Lee

Ruth Legnini
John and Cecily Littleton
Mr. and Mrs. Alan B. Lungren
The McFarlands - Terry, Terri and Claire
Janet MacGaffey
Vickie, Julia and John Mann
Len and Nancy Murphy
Keith Pryor and Mary Geisz
Francisco and Jennifer Robelo
Karen Schloesser
Bryn Smythe
The Wagner Family
The Walls Family
Susan Whereat
Ellen Woodward
The Zakeosian's

Fr. Duffey's favorite 2003 St. George's Chapter:
Wilson DeWald, Donna DiPaulo, Joanne Haley, Bob Hamilton, Cynthia Pound, Sally Ralph and Brian Smith

Recipe Listing

Recipe Listing

Recipe Listing

And Finally!

DAD'S MACARONI AND CHEESE

This is a humorous, tongue-in-cheek recipe, although I definitely drew on my experiences as a new Dad when I wrote it!

Ingredients
1 box macaroni and cheese
Doritos
1 can bean dip
Bruce Springsteen CD

Directions
Find the blue box in the pantry. The dark blue box. The light blue box is instant cocoa. Find a pot with a handle. Fill it with water. Turn the burner on the stove to high. Put the pot on the burner. Wait until bubbles appear.

While you wait, open a bag of Doritos and a can of bean dip. When the bubbles appear, open the box. Remove the white packet and dump the rest of the box in the water. Fish the 25 cents off coupon out of the water. Run cold water over your burnt fingers. Next time use tongs.

Go to the family room and put on Bruce Springsteen CD. Play air guitar to "Born in the USA". Turn off the burner only after noticing that the pot has boiled over. Drain macaroni. This involves pouring the contents of the pot through something with holes in it. If you know where (or what) a colander is, use it. Otherwise make do with a tennis racket, a window screen or holes punched in aluminum foil.

Put macaroni back in the pot. Add contents of the packet (be sure to open it with your teeth), a piece of butter the size of your thumb and a splash of milk. Stir until powder goes away. Serve.

Gloat when your wife makes homemade macaroni and cheese from scratch and the kids say, "I like Daddy's better!"

Michael Fox